the glorious christ

As an apple tree among the trees of the forest,
so is my beloved among the young men.
With great delight I sat in his shadow,
and his fruit was sweet to my taste.
SONG OF SONGS 2:3

the glorious christ

*Meditations on His Person,
Work, and Love*

SECOND EDITION

Kris Lundgaard

P&R
PUBLISHING
P.O. BOX 817 • PHILLIPSBURG • NEW JERSEY 08865-0817

Drawing of The Tree of Life *by Lenka Knoetze*
Cover design by Jelena Mirkovic

ISBN: 979-8-88779-010-7 (pbk)
ISBN: 979-8-88779-011-4 (ePub)

Printed in the United States of America

Library of Congress Cataloging-in-Publication Data has been applied for.

To Karen,
still my princess

contents

list of poems

about this book

This book is about Christ.

It's for those who gaze on Christ as he is displayed in the Scriptures and relish everything about him we can know—all his loveliness and wonder.

It's for anyone who is in awe of Christ and who loves nothing more than to revel in his greatness and wallow in his beauty. It's for lovers of Christ who are so taken with him that they want to lose themselves in thoughts of nothing but the Lamb of God.

It's for people like me who for a long time have had this feeling deep inside that Christ should be everything to them, their highest joy and crown—yet have never been able to keep him in the center of their thoughts.

It's for people who want to be like Christ and try their hardest but fail.

It's for newborn babes in Christ, just tasting the wonder of Christ, learning to take their first steps in adoring him.

It's for lukewarm believers who have lost their first love for Christ—people whose affection for him is a flickering, fading flame.

It's for skeptics who wonder why all the fuss about Christ.

This book is about Christ.

Christ with me, Christ before me, Christ behind me,
Christ in me, Christ beneath me, Christ above me,
Christ on my right, Christ on my left,
Christ when I lie down, Christ when I sit down,
      Christ when I arise.[1]

---

1. From "The Deer's Cry," attributed to St. Patrick, in *Selections from Ancient Irish Poetry*, trans. Kuno Meyer (London: Constable & Company, 1911), 27.

author's note

I've adapted this book from one of John Owen's best-loved works, *Meditations and Discourses on the Glory of Christ.* His meditations are justly treasured by many, and I thank God for Owen's life and writing. Though I've presented his work my way, I've tried to keep Christ's glory central. Christ is the point.

I owe Maria denBoer and Thom Notaro thanks for their editorial nitpicking as I prepared the manuscript of the first edition. Barbara Lerch's unquenchable good cheer made that work pleasant. Amanda Martin has guided and encouraged me through this revision and updating of the text; I especially appreciate her sound judgment and patience as well as the service of painstaking editing that she and Aaron Gottier provided.

My friend Eric Manthei was a careful reader and faithful corrector and commenter as I prepared the revised manuscript. Thanks, Eric—you probably don't realize how important your work has been.

Paula, my bride, remains my favorite reader of all.

God has given Lenka Knoetze the ability to evoke joy with her drawing. Thank you, Lenka, for *The Tree of Life.* It makes me smile.

I still have my notes from a class on the English Puritans taught by J. I. Packer at Reformed Theological Seminary in 1988.

That's where Dr. Packer planted the seeds of my love for John Owen. He also had kind words for my original manuscript and helped me to smooth over a few rough spots. I could use his help now, but he's enjoying that direct vision of our glorious Christ that we all long for.

And Christ, my Lord Jesus Christ, is the glory of it all. I thank you, precious Jesus.

For now we see in a mirror dimly.
—1 Corinthians 13:12

We all, with unveiled face, beholding as in a mirror the glory of the Lord, are being transformed into the same image from glory to glory.
—2 Corinthians 3:18 NKJV

Our faith, therefore, at present beholds God as absent. How so? Because it sees not his face, but rests satisfied with the image in the mirror; but when we shall have left the world, and gone to him, it will behold him as near and before its eyes.
—John Calvin on 1 Corinthians 13:12

Lord, Thou art fulness, I am emptiness:
Yet hear my heart speak in its speechlessness
Extolling Thine unuttered loveliness.
—Christina Rossetti

We start our journey by
discovering two unexpected truths:
There's a glorious Being
who longs for our company, and
by seeing him we will become like him.

1

to see his glory

A lotta cats copy the Mona Lisa,
but people still line up to see the original.
—Louis Armstrong

Designer Imitations

I was drunk the whole first semester. Not Bacchanalian drunk, or even frat-house drunk—that wouldn't do for a seminarian. I was drunk on the depths of God's Word as it was unfolded to my spongy mind all morning and into the midafternoon, every day, five days a week. I had no idea there was so much in the Bible, no idea how exhilarating it could be.

Richard Pratt's literary analysis of historical narrative was opening my eyes daily to the rich and unexpected significance of Abraham's sojourn in Egypt or Ehud's gruesome-yet-comic dispatching of Eglon.[1] I was eager to master Pratt's method and mine my own treasures from the Word. When the school released us for fall break, I went home to Little Rock and was invited (as a "visiting scholar," I suppose) to teach Sunday school. I tried

1. Genesis 12:10–20 and Judges 3:12–30 respectively.

in one hour to unload everything I'd learned from Richard in seven weeks.[2]

In my elevated state, I didn't notice whether anyone was tracking with me. All I knew was that I was giving them the best stuff from my favorite teacher. But I slowly became aware of something odd: I was pacing around the room as I talked. At one point I sat on a table and let my legs dangle over the edge. I started swinging them back and forth.

This wasn't me. Yes, it was my body, my typically tranquil body, but I was possessed by the mannerisms of Richard Pratt—a notorious buzz of peripatetic motion in class. I was unconsciously being conformed to his image.

Why?

When we admire someone, our hearts are warmed and softened. A warm and soft heart is like warm and soft wax, ready to take the imprint or image of something pressed into it, as a seal is pressed into wax. I'm sure you've noticed that when you find a friend you enjoy and admire, your face begins to make new expressions or your voice glides into a new accent. You might even start to laugh with your friend's laugh. Or you might sit on a table and swing your legs, not knowing why.

This happens because God designed us this way. We become like the people and things we love, whether good or evil. From our earliest days we are natural imitators who are shaped by the things we look up to: parents, friends, or heroes. The psalmist is talking about more than mere idols of wood and stone when he says, in Psalm 115,

> Their idols are silver and gold,
>   the work of human hands.

2. I still recommend Dr. Pratt's *He Gave Us Stories: The Bible Student's Guide to Interpreting Old Testament Narratives* (Brentwood, TN: Wolgemuth & Hyatt, 1990; repr., Phillipsburg, NJ: P&R Publishing, 1993).

They have mouths, but do not speak;
>   eyes, but do not see.
They have ears, but do not hear;
>   noses, but do not smell.
They have hands, but do not feel;
>   feet, but do not walk;
>   and they do not make a sound in their throat.
Those who make them become like them;
>   so do all who trust in them. (vv. 4–8)

Simply put, we become what we worship.

So it was only natural, given my admiration of Richard, that I would start becoming more and more like him.

Ultimate Imitations

The Scriptures tell us that, in the end, we who belong to Christ will be like him: "Beloved, we are God's children now, and what we will be has not yet appeared; but we know that when he appears we shall be like him, because we shall see him as he is" (1 John 3:2). We who often live in frustration and weakness will one day become like the Lord Jesus himself. This is a miracle of God's loving grace: even though we through sin disfigured his image, in which he made us in the beginning, God, who is rich in mercy, will through Christ undo our undoing and recreate us in the image of his Son.

That's something to think about. We'll be with him. We'll be like him. Is there any friend more satisfying to be with? Is there any hero you'd rather be like? Is there anything better you can dream of?

But notice *how* it is that we'll become like Christ. Read the end of 1 John 3:2 again: "We shall be like him, *because we shall see him as he is.*" In that day, God will remove the blinders of weakness and sin from our eyes and we will see Christ in all his loveliness and majesty (Isa. 33:17). Because we'll see him clearly, we'll love him completely—for there is nothing unlovely in him. To the limit of our recreated capacity, we'll see the fullness of his nobility, excellence, holiness, righteousness, kindness, mercy, goodness—every beauty that could make us cherish him. And that fundamental principle in us, that we become what we worship, will be fulfilled. Adoring him wholeheartedly, with nothing to hinder us, we will be like him.

Our Dying Lord's Longing

In just a few hours, you will die in agony. What's worse, you already know it, and you know that no governor in heaven or on earth will stay your execution. Your friends are gathered around you for a meal, which you know will be your last together before you're torn from them. What's more, you know that when the end comes, all of them will desert you.

That is what Christ faced. Of course, none of us could fill his shoes, but if I were in his place, I would have wallowed in self-pity. I couldn't have held back the resentment that would have swept over me as I looked into the eyes of those who would soon betray, deny, and desert me.

But consider our Lord's words at the table:

> Let not your hearts be troubled. Believe in God; believe also in me. In my Father's house are many rooms. If it were not so, would I have told you that I go to prepare a place for you? And if I go and prepare a place for you, I will come again and will take you to myself, that where I am you may be also. (John 14:1–3)

No chiding or resentment, no self-pity or self-absorption—only concern for his friends and a tender longing to be with them.

John 14:3 should make us fall prostrate, dumbstruck and incredulous. This is the Lord of glory talking, the matchless King of the universe who could have anything his heart desires, and he's talking about going home to fix up some rooms in his palace so his friends can come and stay with him. Jesus has shown love to his people in countless ways, but is any more marked by human affection than this?

Wanting to have his friends with him forever, Jesus later that evening turns to the Father to offer up his fragrant longings, just as the high priest offered incense in the temple. He restates his love for us as he makes a startling request: "Father, I desire that they also, whom you have given me, may be with me where I am, to see my glory that you have given me because you loved me before the foundation of the world" (John 17:24).

Someone who doesn't know Jesus might read this verse and think him awfully taken with himself. But those who know Jesus rejoice at his request. We know that to be with him and to see his glory are all that can satisfy us—all that can bring us peace. Without these, no soul can truly rest. As a needle that's rubbed against a magnet and placed on a floating cork will twist and bob until it finds north, the heart of the believer, having tasted the love of Christ, will not rest until it lands in his embracing arms (Song 2:6). "You have made us for yourself, and our heart is restless till it finds its rest in you."[3]

When I found myself turning into a Richard Pratt impersonator, something more was at work than my admiration for him—something else was accelerating my transformation: The one I admired was also returning my affection. Richard didn't use his office hours to keep students at arm's length. He wanted us to call him Richard (school policy notwithstanding). To paraphrase

3. Augustine, *The Confessions*, trans. Philip Burton (New York: Alfred A. Knopf, 2001), 1.1.

Jesus in John 15:15, he no longer called us students but called us friends. When an ice storm left the seminary without electricity for a week, Richard and his wife Gina hosted three of us students and our families; during our stay, Richard would get out his guitar and lead us in family worship around his fireplace. When his unexpected affection met my admiration for him, nothing in me could resist the impulse to become like him.

In the same way, the tenderness Christ shows us draws us to him and impels our hearts to be like him.

Two Ways of Seeing

Jesus asks the Father to let us see his glory. This request wells up from his love, because he knows that to see him is our greatest joy and gift—not just in the world to come, but now. It's the life and reward of our souls. When we see him, we see the Father (John 14:9). In the face of Christ, we see "the light of the knowledge of the glory of God" (2 Cor. 4:6). And as we reflect on him, we are transformed into his image: "But we all, with unveiled face, *beholding as in a mirror the glory of the Lord*, are being transformed into the same image from glory to glory" (2 Cor. 3:18 NKJV).

The Scriptures distinguish two ways or degrees of seeing the glory of Christ. Paul makes this distinction when he says, "We walk by faith, not by sight" (2 Cor. 5:7). He is contrasting our lives "at home in the body" and "away from the Lord" (2 Cor. 5:6) with our lives in the world to come. In both, our joy is to contemplate the beauty of Christ. In this world we see his reflection "in a mirror dimly," because we see him only by faith; in the world to come we'll see him "face to face" (1 Cor. 13:12).

In John 17, Jesus longs for his people to be with him and to see his glory. Although he prays that our vision of his glory will be perfected in heaven, he doesn't ignore the sight of his glory that we can have by faith now. And when we return his love, we of course want to know how we can see his glory now.

What Glory Can the Eyes of Faith See?

When Jesus walked with his disciples on earth, they saw "his glory, glory as of the only Son from the Father, full of grace and truth" (John 1:14). But what glory did they see, and how did they see it? They couldn't have seen the eternal glory of his deity, because no one can see that in this world (1 Tim. 1:17). Nor did they see the splendor of an earthly kingdom, for Christ "emptied himself, by taking the form of a servant" (Phil. 2:7). He would have been more easily mistaken for a slave than for a king. He had no place to lay his head (Matt. 8:20), much less a palace. And the disciples didn't see his glory shining in a handsome face: according to the Scriptures, the Savior didn't save anyone with his good looks.

> As many were astonished at you—
> > his appearance was so marred, beyond human semblance,
> > and his form beyond that of the children of mankind—
>
> . . . .
> he had no form or majesty that we should look at him,
> > and no beauty that we should desire him.
> He was despised and rejected by men,
> > a man of sorrows and acquainted with grief;
> and as one from whom men hide their faces
> > he was despised, and we esteemed him not. (Isa. 52:14;
> > 53:2–3)

How, then, did they see his glory? They saw his glory as the one "full of grace and truth" (John 1:14). That is, they saw he was the Promised One who had come to bring the grace and truth of God to his people. And they saw this only by faith, because the only ones who saw this glory were those who received him and "believed in his name" (John 1:12). They saw the glory of the "Lamb of God, who takes away the sin of the world" (John 1:29). This is the same glory we can see by faith today.

When we look on Christ by faith and see him as he is revealed in the Word, we love him more. Each view of him draws us deeper into delight. As John Owen puts it, "Herein would I live; herein would I die; hereon would I dwell in my thoughts and affections, to the withering and consumption of all the painted beauties of this world, unto the crucifying all things here below, until they become unto me a dead and deformed thing, no way meet for affectionate embraces."[4]

The Treasures before Us

Anything that Christ prays for must be good. When he prays for us to see his glory, we know there's something extraordinary in store for us. As we begin to reflect on the beauty of his glory, we'll find a trove of treasures before us.

Gazing on Christ Gives Rest, Satisfaction, and Peace to Our Souls

Our minds tend to be full of perplexed thoughts; fears, cares, distresses, passions, and lusts throw us into disorder, darkness, and confusion. But when our best thoughts are fixed on Jesus,[5] our hearts will be kept holy, serene, and spiritual, for "to be spiritually minded is life and peace" (Rom. 8:6 NKJV). Reflecting

---

4. John Owen, *Meditations and Discourses on the Glory of Christ*, reprinted in *The Works of John Owen*, ed. William H. Goold, vol. 1 (Edinburgh: Johnstone & Hunter, 1850; repr., Banner of Truth Trust, 1991), 291.

5. See Colossians 3:1–17, especially verses 1 and 15; also Hebrews 12:2–3.

on Christ takes our minds off things below—things that aren't worth comparing to the great worth, beauty, and glory that we see in him (Phil. 3:7–11). When we take our eyes off Christ, we become strangers to heavenly life, and we live without the spiritual refreshment and satisfaction that God offers in his gospel.

Admiring Christ Makes Us Like Him

If I couldn't help becoming like Richard when I was taken with his skilled teaching and sincere friendship, how could I by faith take a real look at the wonder of Christ without being changed into his likeness according to his promise (2 Cor. 3:18)? If we have been touched by God's grace and truly know him, we can't escape the transforming power of a glimpse of our beloved Lord.

Adoring Christ Whets Our Appetite for Heaven

We know that in heaven we'll be filled with joy forever. But what will be the fountain of that joy? Seeing the glory of our Lord Jesus. The Scriptures repeatedly assure us of this future treasure.

> Then we who are alive, who are left, will be caught up together with them in the clouds to meet the Lord in the air, and so we will always be with the Lord. Therefore encourage one another with these words. (1 Thess. 4:17–18)

> My desire is to depart and be with Christ, for that is far better. (Phil. 1:23)

To be with him is far better than our earthly lives because we'll see his glory (John 17:24), and, by seeing him as he is, "we shall be like him" (1 John 3:2). This is the goal of our salvation and will be our joy forever.

The beatific vision—an unhindered sight of God—is the eternal fountain that gives life to souls in heaven. But we know that the immense and infinite essence of God is invisible to the eyes of our flesh. In fact, we'll never be able to see the essence of God, because we are and will always be finite creatures. So the sight that we'll have of God will always be "in the face of Jesus Christ" (2 Cor. 4:6). In Christ alone we'll see the glory of God in his infinite perfection, and this vision will fill us with peace, rest, and joy.

We can admire these things here, but we can't comprehend them. When we talk about seeing the perfection of God in Christ, we're high in the Himalayas of thought, walking a knife-edge. We have to choose our words as carefully as we would our steps on that precipice, lest we stumble. Still, believers have in Christ a foresight and foretaste of this ultimate vision of God. We sometimes hold in our hearts, by the Word and the Spirit, a sense of the unaltered glory of God shining out from Christ, which moves and saturates our souls with unspeakable joy. From this comes "the peace of God, which surpasses all understanding" (Phil. 4:7). Christ, our "hope of glory" (Col. 1:27), gives us a taste of the firstfruits of his heaven. Sometimes he even lets us bathe our souls in his light and drink of the rivers of pleasure that are at his right hand (Ps. 16:11).

The wonders of Christ lie before us. Even though we see but a poor reflection of him (1 Cor. 13:12), what we can see and know of him will calm our souls, stir our hunger for him, and make us like him. I pray that through the following chapters our Beloved himself will woo us with his beauty and grant us the grace to surrender to him as we feast on *the glorious Christ*.

For Reflection and Discussion

1. Christ is the Bridegroom of the church, his beautiful bride. With this in mind, answer the question that is posed in Song of Songs 5:9: "What is your beloved more than another beloved,

O most beautiful among women?" (In other words, what is it that you love about Christ? Be as specific as you can.)

2. Have you ever felt unusually close to Christ and in some sense received a foretaste of heaven as you gazed on him by faith? If so, describe one or two things about Christ that you were taken with.

3. What are your expectations as you begin this journey? Make a list of at least three things you'd like God to do in, to, or for you. Now ask him to do them—for the glory of Christ.

That Where I Am, There Ye May Be Also

How know I that it looms lovely that land I have never seen,
With morning-glories and heartsease and unexampled green,
With neither heat nor cold in the balm-redolent air?
    Some of this, not all, I know; but this is so;
        Christ is there.

How know I that blessedness befalls who dwell in Paradise,
The outwearied hearts refreshing, rekindling the worn-out
        eyes,
All souls singing, seeing, rejoicing everywhere?
    Nay, much more than this I know; for this is so;
        Christ is there.

O Lord Christ, whom having not seen I love and desire to
        love,
O Lord Christ, who lookest on me uncomely yet still Thy
        dove,
Take me to Thee in Paradise, Thine own made fair;
    For whatever else I know, this thing is so;
        Thou art there.

CHRISTINA ROSSETTI

Chapters 2 through 10 are a long stretch of breathtaking vistas.
Each chapter is a scenic overlook where we'll stop and gaze at yet another beautiful side of Christ.

2

the only face of God

Was never face so pleased my mind.
—Anonymous

The Truth about Emeth

C. S. Lewis has been the most influential writer in my life. Perhaps you could say the same. Yet in the last book of his Chronicles of Narnia, he takes a path I cannot follow. Near the end of Narnian history, Emeth[1] meets his Maker, Aslan, the great Lion who is the Christ figure of Narnia. The name *Aslan* had been hateful to him during his life, because Emeth had worshiped the rival god Tash. But after he meets Aslan, Emeth sings a different tune. As he describes the encounter to King Peter and others, he says that when he saw Aslan approaching, he was undone.

> Then I fell at his feet and thought, Surely this is the hour of death. . . . But the Glorious One bent down his golden head and touched my forehead with his tongue and said,

1. His name sounds like the Hebrew word for *truth*.

31

Son, thou art welcome. But I said, Alas, Lord, I am no son of Thine, but the servant of Tash. He answered, Child, all the service thou hast done to Tash, I account as service done to me. . . . Dost thou understand, Child? I said, Lord, thou knowest how much I understand. But I said also (for the truth constrained me), Yet I have been seeking Tash all my days. Beloved, said the Glorious One, unless thy desire had been for me thou wouldst not have sought so long and so truly. For all find what they truly seek.[2]

Lewis is offering an answer to the hard question of what happens to those who live and die without having ever known the name of Jesus. He suggests, if I read him right, that some might serve Christ unwittingly—even in the name of a false god—but that, because their service is counted by God as really to Christ, they will be received into his eternal kingdom.

I'm not a theologian and can't fully critique Lewis. I don't know what Scriptures and reasoning lie behind his story of Emeth. Still, although I admit that the destiny of the souls who never hear the gospel is a tough question, I can't be happy with any answer that implies that Christ isn't essential. Jesus and his apostles go out of their way to make clear that Christ alone is the way to know God.

Truly, truly, I say to you, he who does not enter the sheepfold by the door but climbs in by another way, that man is a thief and a robber. . . .

I am the door. If anyone enters by me, he will be saved. (John 10:1, 9)

---

2. C. S. Lewis, *The Last Battle* (New York: Macmillan, 1956), 156–57. This is, even with what I believe to be a flaw, a beautiful book.

No one comes to the Father except through me. (John 14:6)

Whoever has seen me has seen the Father. (John 14:9)

For God, who said, "Let light shine out of darkness," has shone in our hearts to give the light of the knowledge of the glory of God in the face of Jesus Christ. (2 Cor. 4:6)

Peter says explicitly that salvation is only in the *name* of Christ: "And there is salvation in no one else, for there is no other name under heaven given among men by which we must be saved" (Acts 4:12).

Only Christ can show us God: this is the first way we know his glory. In the face of Christ, the church can see the nature of God, the divine person of the Father. Without Christ, we can know and see nothing of it. In Christ alone, we know the terror and beauty of who God is and the unsearchable wisdom of his unfathomable mind. Whatever sketchy, imperfect notions we may discover about God in his creation, apart from Christ we can't have the "light of the knowledge of the glory of God" that enlightens our minds and purifies our hearts. To know God, we must see him in "Christ, who is the image of God" (2 Cor. 4:4), because the Son "is the radiance of the glory of God and the exact imprint of his nature" (Heb. 1:3). "He is the image of the invisible God" (Col. 1:15).

It is Christ's glory to be the unique representative to us of God's nature and will; had he not come, God would have been forever invisible to us. "No one has ever seen God; the only God, who is at the Father's side, he has made him known" (John 1:18). Because he is God, the Son has always been the image of the Father. He is in the Father, and the Father is in him; they are unified in the one divine essence (John 14:10). When he became man, he became the face of God to the church (2 Cor. 4:6)—the "visible

God." This is the glory Christ had with the Father before the world existed (John 17:5) and that by faith we may taste and see.

And this is why Emeth's story troubles me. If he can come to Aslan through Tash, is Lewis suggesting that someone could come to Christ through a mere idol? Christ says no. The apostles say no. In truth, if we could just as easily know God through a false religion, Christ is no more glorious than a golden calf.

How Was God Known before Christ Came?

Before the incarnation, God's people knew him through the revelation of his Word and the ceremonies of his worship. This was the glory and privilege of Israel (Ps. 147:19–20; Rom. 9:4). God's people knew him, but they knew him as the one who lived in "thick darkness" (Ex. 20:21; Deut. 5:22; 1 Kings 8:12; 2 Chron. 6:1). God represented himself in darkness to teach them about the glory that he would later uncover in Christ. But now, in the face of Christ, we see that "God is light, and in him is no darkness at all" (1 John 1:5).

When the Son of God appeared in the flesh, all the mysteries of God—his being, his existence in three persons, all the glorious properties of his divine nature—were extravagantly displayed to everyone who believed. And the light of the knowledge of them obliterated every shadow in the church and blazed into the darkness that covered the world, so that no one continued to be ignorant of God except those who refused to see (John 1:5, 14, 17–18; 2 Cor. 4:3–4).

The deepest longing of those who are closest to God has always been to see his glory. David yearned and prayed to see God, although he could see him only in types and shadows.

> O God, you are my God; earnestly I seek you;
>   my soul thirsts for you;

my flesh faints for you,
> as in a dry and weary land where there is no water.
So I have looked upon you in the sanctuary,
> beholding your power and glory. (Ps. 63:1–2)

God gave glimpses of his glory in the sanctuary, or in the ceremonies of worship,[3] and David devoured those rare delicacies. Now that we see his glory with unveiled faces, though still as in a mirror (2 Cor. 3:18), how much more should we cherish such a view!

But how do we behold his glory? If we're left to ourselves, if we have no other hope but to try to raise our thoughts by their own bootstraps to the immensity of the divine nature, we'll grasp and flounder with Agur:

Surely I am too stupid to be a man.
> I have not the understanding of a man.
I have not learned wisdom,
> nor have I knowledge of the Holy One.
Who has ascended to heaven and come down?
> Who has gathered the wind in his fists?
Who has wrapped up the waters in a garment?
> Who has established all the ends of the earth?
What is his name, and what is his son's name?
> Surely you know! (Prov. 30:2–4)

But in his kindness God appointed his Son to be his face to us. Let's turn to his face—and let's start by reflecting on just two aspects of the beauty of God that we see in Christ. In these we can see that Christ is *the only face of God*.

3. For a detailed discussion of how Christ was prefigured in Old Testament worship and law, see Vern S. Poythress, *The Shadow of Christ in the Law of Moses* (Brentwood, TN: Wolgemuth & Hyatt, 1991; repr., Phillipsburg, NJ: P&R Publishing, 1995).

In Christ's Face, We See the Wisdom of God

> But where shall wisdom be found?
> And where is the place of understanding? (Job 28:12)

> Can you find out the deep things of God?
> Can you find out the limit of the Almighty? (Job 11:7)

We can't see God's wisdom in its pure essence, but we can begin to sound its depths by studying his works. And his most excellent work is his devising the salvation of the church. That's why Paul celebrates his calling

> to preach to the Gentiles the unsearchable riches of Christ, and to bring to light for everyone what is the plan of the mystery hidden for ages in God, who created all things, so that through the church the manifold wisdom of God might now be made known to the rulers and authorities in the heavenly places. (Eph. 3:8–10)

In the beginning it seemed that Satan had outwitted God (Gen. 3). By a clever deception he persuaded Adam and Eve, God's crowning creation, to rebel against his loving rule. The result was death and decay that buried the world under its ugly weight, until all creation groaned for deliverance (Rom. 8:20–22). God could have overcome Satan by mere strength; he could have melted him with one blast of his holy breath. But how would that have vindicated God's wisdom? The question would have lingered: Who is cleverer? Satan, who craftily upended God's plan with deceit, or God, who resorted to mere force to crush his enemy?

When we trace the thread of God's plan as it is uncovered in Christ, we can't help but cheer as God makes a fool of his chief enemy. Satan and his demonic horde probably partied from the kiss of Judas until the stone over the tomb began to tremble. They were clueless—otherwise they never would have crucified the Lord of glory (1 Cor. 2:8). We see God's wisdom in how he patiently waited to send Christ to the rescue at just the right time (Rom. 5:6; Gal. 4:4–5). We marvel at how he resolved the problem of bringing filthy, fallen creatures back into his holy presence (1 Peter 3:18).

If we have any interest in God, if we hope for the joy of gazing on his glory through all eternity, how can we help but hunger for a taste of the delicious wisdom of God in this life? All the treasures of this wisdom are laid up and laid out in "Christ the ... wisdom of God" (1 Cor. 1:24). And when we see the infinite wisdom of God in Christ, we see *Christ's* glory—the glory given him by his Father. For this is his glory: that in him alone we see the depth and breadth of the wisdom of God. It's true that all of creation plainly declares God's wisdom (Ps. 19:1–6)—yet its voice is but a whisper compared to the thundering shout of God's wisdom in Jesus.

To see this wisdom clearly in Christ is *our* wisdom. Deep reflection on it fills our souls "with joy that is inexpressible and filled with glory" (1 Peter 1:8).

In Christ's Face We See the Love of God

"God is love" (1 John 4:8). His eternal nature is love. But what do we see in the world? That the "wrath of God is revealed from heaven against all ungodliness and unrighteousness of men" (Rom. 1:18). The world is filled with evidence of his anger and displeasure, so how can we know and see the glory of the God who is love? "In this the love of God was made manifest among us, that God sent his only Son into the world, so that we might live through him" (1 John 4:9).

The Father gave this glory to Christ: With his blood he would write in large letters that *God is love.* For our sake alone, and under no other compulsion than his affection for us, he took on our flesh. He gladly despised shame and humiliation that he didn't deserve. He bared his back for the whip, bowed his head for the ignominious crown, and stretched out his hands to receive the nails. All this for us. All this in love. And all this so that "in everything he might be preeminent" (Col. 1:18).

Do you see how excellent, how beautiful, how desirable he is? In him we have the most joyful sight of God that any creature can see. Any notion of God's goodness that we can glean from nature or his providence is precious, yet it does not tell us that *God is love.* By declaring that God is love, Christ is glorious.

The Treasure Hidden in the Field

These brief meditations have only pointed to Christ's glory in his role as God's face to us; we've seen two grainy snapshots of God's wisdom and love as they are displayed in him. But God made a promise, through Isaiah, to establish a new covenant in which our "eyes will behold the king in his beauty" (Isa. 33:17)—we will gaze on the glory of Christ in all its luster and magnificence.

To reflect on this beauty of the King of saints is the work of faith. And who can measure this privilege: that we who were born in darkness and deserved to be cast out into utter darkness have been transported into this marvelous "light of the knowledge of the glory of God in the face of Jesus Christ"? What are all the stained glories, the fading beauties, of this world? Pile them all in a bucket and weigh them in the balance against one glimpse of God's face in Christ, and they are nothing—his beauty surpasses "all that is in the world, even as the rose in bloom surpasses the dust of the desert."[4]

4. To borrow from Emeth's praise of Aslan. Lewis, *The Last Battle*, 155–56.

He is wonderful.

Another wonder, but of a different kind, is that we give little time to admiring our glorious Christ. It seems beyond us. Thoughts of his glory are too high or too deep for us. We won't stretch our faith to reach up to them or dig down into them. When a dear image of Christ as our tender Bridegroom takes the stage of our minds, we are so easily, so quickly distracted. Within a few minutes we weary of glimpses of Christ, even though such visions are meant to feed our souls through all eternity.

Could it be that our minds are tuned to another frequency? We're accustomed to easier diversions and aren't in shape for the faith-work of reflecting on Christ. That may be why some of us live at low spiritual tide, as passive and joyless disciples.

But if we were in love with Christ, so that we couldn't wait to see him again, and if we were in the habit of gazing on him and marveling at him, then our lives before God would be sweeter to us. Day by day our spirits would grow stronger. We would more faithfully represent Christ to the world. Strange as it sounds, death might start to sound inviting to us, but only as the final release from everything that distracts us from the sight of our Lord.

We must prize seeing the glory of God in the face of Christ as the greatest privilege in this life. It is the dawn of heaven and the firstfruits of eternal life; in fact, this is eternal life—that we may know the only true God as well as Jesus Christ, whom he sent (John 17:3). Unless we esteem it, we won't enjoy it; and anything we don't value according to its worth we despise. It's not enough for us to consider it a privilege and an advantage; we must value it above *everything*. Our souls must yearn and faint for it; our hearts and our flesh have to cry out for a taste of the living God (Ps. 84:2), or we'll be forever a stranger to his glory.

C. S. Lewis may have slipped in his attempt to rescue those who never hear the gospel, but he knew the glory of Christ. He knew that Christ was the bright Morning Star—the only face of God to us: "We must think of the Son always, so to speak, streaming forth from the Father, like light from a lamp, or heat from a fire, or thoughts from a mind. He is the self-expression of the Father—what the Father has to say. And there never was a time when He was not saying it."[5]

For Reflection and Discussion

1. Christ is the Bridegroom of the church, his beautiful bride. With that in mind, answer the question that is posed in Song of Songs 5:9: "What is your beloved more than another beloved, O most beautiful among women?" (Yes, you've seen this question before. You'll see it again. And again. Each time you see it, try to answer it based on your reflections from the current chapter.)

2. Read Exodus 33. What can you learn from Moses about getting a view of the glory of God?

3. One reason we don't gaze more often on the glory of God in the face of Christ is that we don't know how. John Owen suggests that we might have something to learn from our "vicious habits"—our ruminations on worldly things that lead our minds and hearts away from God. Take some time to examine what carries your mind away (be careful here—try to be specific without stirring up unhealthy thoughts and soiling your conscience). How do you feed that unhelpful hunger in your imagination? Write down a few thoughts. Is there anything you can turn right side up and use to help you to be carried away instead by the glory of Christ?

---

5. C. S. Lewis, *Mere Christianity* (New York: MacMillan, 1952), 135.

4. List at least five aspects of the way God worked out our salvation in Christ (such as appointing a Mediator who was both God and man). How does each of them show his wisdom?

5. Read one or more of the following stories from the life of Christ: Matthew 9:1–8; 12:1–14, 22–37; 21:23–27. For each episode, describe how Christ showed his wisdom and how his wisdom is supreme.

6. Using your answer to question 4 or 5, compose a prayer to Christ that praises him for revealing the wisdom of God. You may want to fashion your prayer in the form of "narrative praise," as modeled in Exodus 15:1–18, by telling Christ a story of his own greatness.[6]

---

6. For some helpful instruction on how to do this, see Richard L. Pratt, Jr., *Pray with Your Eyes Open* (Phillipsburg, NJ: Presbyterian and Reformed, 1987), chapter 4.

3

lost in a mystery

I love to lose myself in a mystery;
to pursue my reason to an O altitudo!¹

—SIR THOMAS BROWNE

Who Is the God of the Storm?

Religions must answer a basic question: Who is the god who brings the rain to water the earth and feed his creatures? On Mount Carmel, when Elijah had his showdown with the prophets of Baal, this was the disputed point (1 Kings 18:16–46). The God of Israel had withheld rain for years and dried up the land because of the sins of the people, but now he wanted to reveal his power. He had Elijah challenge the prophets of Baal to a duel to see who could bring fire from heaven. Four hundred fifty prophets of Baal prayed their hearts out, sacrificed a bull, danced until they dropped, slashed themselves with swords and spears, and shouted themselves hoarse. They begged Baal, their

---

1. *O altitudo* is the Latin exclamation that begins the Vulgate version of Romans 11:33: "Oh, the depth of the riches and wisdom and knowledge of God!" It expresses how Paul was swept away by wonder as he swam in the depths of God's wisdom.

presumptive god of the storm, to send a thunderbolt to burn the offering on their altar. But the only sound they heard was Elijah's taunting.

When Elijah prayed to his God, a firebolt fell from heaven and consumed his offering—and the altar itself. Then "the heavens grew black with clouds and wind, and there was a great rain" (1 Kings 18:45).

Again and again, the Old Testament declares and shows the God of Israel to be the God of the storm:

> The floods have lifted up, O LORD,
> > the floods have lifted up their voice;
> > the floods lift up their roaring.
> Mightier than the thunders of many waters,
> > mightier than the waves of the sea,
> > the LORD on high is mighty! (Ps. 93:3–4)

> Then they cried to the LORD in their trouble,
> > and he delivered them from their distress.
> He made the storm be still,
> > and the waves of the sea were hushed.
> Then they were glad that the waters were quiet,
> > and he brought them to their desired haven. (Ps. 107:28–30)[2]

There's no debate: the God of the Old Testament is the God of the storm.

The Kitten or the Thunderstorm?

Jesus's disciples had no idea what they were in for when they followed him into the boat in Matthew 8:23–27. When a

---

2. See also Psalms 29:3, 10; 65:7.

storm swept down on the lake and the waves threatened to sink them, they looked death in the face and their knees knocked. Somehow Jesus was asleep in the boat; they woke him and begged him to save them. Jesus stood up. Without praying to anyone, he spoke to the storm. And the wind wilted, and the sea turned to glass.

Now the disciples were *really* scared. Who was this in the boat with them? These faithful Jewish believers knew the Scriptures and had no doubts about the identity of the God of the storm. Five minutes earlier, they had seen this Jesus as someone much like them asleep in the boat. But now, Matthew tells us, "The men were amazed and asked, 'What sort of man is this, that even winds and sea obey him?'" (v. 27).

I need to take you back to Narnia once more, because there's a passage in the first of the Chronicles that captures the confusion these men must have felt. It's just after the resurrection of Aslan (the lion whom, you recall, is the Christ figure), as he appears to the two girls, Lucy and Susan.

"Oh, children," said the Lion, "I feel my strength coming back to me. Oh, children, catch me if you can!" He stood for a second, his eyes very bright, his limbs quivering, lashing himself with his tail. Then he made a leap high over their heads and landed on the other side of the Table. Laughing, though she didn't know why, Lucy scrambled over to reach him. Aslan leaped again. A mad chase began. Round and round the hill-top he led them, now hopelessly out of their reach, now letting them almost catch his tail, now diving between them, now tossing them in the air with his huge and beautifully velveted paws and catching them again, and now stopping unexpectedly so that all three of them rolled over together in a happy laughing heap of fur and arms and legs. It was such a romp as no one has ever had except in Narnia;

and whether it was more like playing with a thunderstorm or playing with a kitten Lucy never could make up her mind.[3]

The kitten or the thunderstorm? Is Jesus man, or is he God? Is he our friend—made of the same stuff as we are, walking beside us, struggling under the weakness of human flesh as we are—or is he enthroned above the heavens, all-powerful, awesome, terrible, sovereign?

The Bible answers *yes*.

In Christ—in one person—there are two distinct natures. One is eternal, infinite, immense, almighty—the form and essence of God; the other begins in time and is finite, limited, and confined to a certain place. This second nature is ours, and he assumed it when he "became flesh and dwelt among us" (John 1:14). There's no one else like him, and in this mystery he is glorious. In fact, this glory of his blazes so brightly that the blind world can't bear its beauty. Most deny the incarnation of the Son of God.

This is the glory that the angels bend down to get a glimpse of (1 Peter 1:12). This glory is the foundation of the church (Matt. 16:16–19). Yet we can't explain it to our children. We run short of words and analogies. Here we have to fall down and worship the Author of this wonderful mystery and, submitting our understanding to the obedience of faith, humbly adore what we can't comprehend.

O Altitudo!

My purpose here isn't to detail the nuances of the mystery of Christ as the God-man. I trust you to explore it as you deepen

3. C. S. Lewis, *The Lion, The Witch, and The Wardrobe* (New York: Macmillan, 1950), 133. The emphasis is mine.

your knowledge of him.[4] My business now is to stir up your mind to contemplate the glory of Christ as God and man in one person. Here are a few prompts to prime your meditations.

Recognize the All-Surpassing Excellence of This Truth

That Christ is both God and man is the best—the most noble, useful, beneficial—subject you could explore. This holy secret is one subject that satisfies all the criteria of Philippians 4:8. What is everything else compared to knowing Christ? Loss and rubbish, in Paul's eyes (Phil. 3:8–10). Fix this truth in your heart and mind.

What do most people think about and long for? According to the psalmist, "Many are asking, 'Who will show us some good?'" (Ps. 4:6). That is, most people want to know who will help them to get the things of this world and give them comfort and happiness and peace of mind. But the psalmist says, "Lift up the light of your face upon us, O Lord! You have put more joy in my heart than they have when their grain and wine abound" (vv. 6–7). Nothing in this world can compare with seeing the light of God's glory in the face of the eternal God-man.

Consider the desirable things of this life: wives or husbands, children, friends, security, health, possessions, and honor. Is anyone indifferent to these? But anyone who catches the least glimpse of the glory of Christ the God-man will say, "Whom have I in heaven but you? And there is nothing on earth that I desire besides you" (Ps. 73:25).

4. A good book can help you if you aren't acquainted with Christian teaching about the person of Christ. I list a few in the "For Reflection and Discussion" section at the end of this chapter. And you'll be well rewarded if you have the patience to work through John Owen's *ΧΡΙΣΤΟΛΟΓΙΑ: or, a Declaration of the Glorious Mystery of the Person of Christ—God and Man*, reprinted in *The Works of John Owen*, ed. William H. Goold, vol. 1 (Edinburgh: Johnstone & Hunter, 1850; repr., Banner of Truth Trust, 1991), 1–272.

Others aren't consumed by the flesh but enjoy the wonder of God's creation and providence, and so they should. Yet this falls short, because even creation and providence have nothing to compare to the glory of the mysterious God-man. Think of the masterful handiwork God displays in the galaxies and atoms; let the wonder of how he directs history according to his plan carry you away. But don't stop there. Come farther up and farther in: lift your thoughts to Christ as God and man.

Discover How Scripture Reveals Christ's Glory as the God-Man

We can't see Christ's glory as the God-man by the mere creativity of our imagination; rather, we see his glory with the vision of faith as we diligently search God's revelation. Consider the example set by the saints of the Old Testament.

> Concerning this salvation, the prophets who prophesied about the grace that was to be yours searched and inquired carefully, inquiring what person or time the Spirit of Christ in them was indicating when he predicted the sufferings of Christ and the subsequent glories. It was revealed to them that they were serving not themselves but you, in the things that have now been announced to you through those who preached the good news to you by the Holy Spirit sent from heaven, things into which angels long to look. (1 Peter 1:10–12)

We must keep this principle in mind no matter which page of the Bible we're reading: the revelation of Christ and his work is the foundation of everything the prophets and apostles say to strengthen us (Eph. 2:20–22). This is what Jesus taught on the road to Emmaus.

And he said to them, "O foolish ones, and slow of heart to believe all that the prophets have spoken! Was it not necessary that the Christ should suffer these things and enter into his glory?"

... Then he opened their minds to understand the Scriptures. (Luke 24:25–26, 45)

There are enough revelations of Christ treasured up in the Scriptures from beginning to end to exercise our faith and fill our meditations until the end of time.

There are three ways in which the Scriptures represent the glory of Christ to us. First, they offer direct descriptions of his glorious person and incarnation.[5] Second, they present innumerable prophecies, promises, and explicit instructions concerning him and displaying his glory for our reflection.[6] Third, the Scriptures show the glory of Christ through the sacred ceremonies of divine worship that were instituted under the Old Testament, as we'll see in chapter 8.[7]

Consider one example from the Old Testament: Isaiah's vision.

In the year that King Uzziah died I saw the LORD sitting upon a throne, high and lifted up; and the train of his robe filled the temple. Above him stood the seraphim. Each had six wings: with two he covered his face, and with two he covered his feet, and with two he flew. And one called to another and said:

5. See, among other places, Genesis 3:15; Psalms 2:7–9; 45:2–6; 68:17–18; 110; Isaiah 6:1–4; 9:6; Zechariah 3:8; John 1:1–3; Philippians 2:6–8; Hebrews 1:1–3; 2:14–16; Revelation 1:17–18.

6. For example, Genesis 49:10; 1 Samuel 2:10; Job 19:25; Psalms 40:6–10 (compare these verses with what Hebrews 10:5–10 says about them); 118:22–26; Isaiah 11:1–10; 40:11; 42:1–4; 49:1–12; 55:3–5; 59:16–20; Jeremiah 23:5–6; 33:15–18; Daniel 7:13–14; Haggai 2:7; Malachi 4:2.

7. The book of Hebrews is our primary guide to the pictures of Christ in Levitical worship.

"Holy, holy, holy is the Lord of hosts;
the whole earth is full of his glory!" (Isa. 6:1–3)

Isaiah saw the glory of the divine presence filling the temple; John tells us that Isaiah saw Christ's glory, revealed later as his divine glory filling the temple of his human body (John 12:41). And if this shadow of glory was so wondrous and holy that the seraphs covered their faces, how much more glorious is it in itself, as it is plainly displayed in the gospel!

Hunt for these visions of Christ's glory as you would for a pearl of great price (Matt. 13:45–46). The Scriptures are the field in which the pearl has been hidden. Every truth in the Bible is for the good of our souls and is a pearl to make us richer, but the most precious pearl shows us the glory of Christ. When we uncover it, we cling to it with joy. To use another metaphor, when we find food for our souls in the Word of truth, we taste how gracious the Lord is. The Scriptures are as refreshing to our hearts as a spring of water is to our bodies.

Think Often of Christ as the God-Man

When we don't think often of Christ as the God-man, our spirits atrophy and we forget the privileges offered to us in the gospel. We confess the doctrines of Christ but rarely meditate on them. In order to meditate on the glory of Christ, our minds must be disciplined to set aside the things of this world. Some of us are strangers to this kind of meditation because we don't trouble ourselves to put our flesh to death (Rom. 8:6, 13).[8]

---

8. For help with this, see my *The Enemy Within: Straight Talk about the Power and Defeat of Sin*, rev. ed. (Phillipsburg, NJ: P&R Publishing, 2023). Or go straight to Owen's writings on sin in *The Works of John Owen*, ed. William H. Goold, vol. 6 (Edinburgh: Johnstone & Hunter, 1851; repr., Banner of Truth Trust, 1991).

Suppose I claim to want nothing more than to see Christ's glory in heaven forever, yet I never stop to meditate on Christ here and now. Does that make sense? My indifference to the glory of Christ that is revealed in the Scriptures is incompatible with true longing to behold Christ and his glory in heaven. And why would I postpone the pleasure I can find in him until heaven, when he offers a taste of himself now?

Don't Go Long without Thoughts of Christ as the God-Man

Christ is near us, even within our hearts (Rom. 10:6–8). When we turn to him, we find him ready to commune with us; that is, as we deepen our knowledge of Christ by reading and meditating on the Word, we may have spontaneous, refreshing thoughts of him throughout the day. And to let us know how near he is and how tenderly he longs to commune with us, he says, "Behold, I stand at the door and knock. If anyone hears my voice and opens the door, I will come in to him and eat with him, and he with me" (Rev. 3:20).

But sometimes, to test our faith or because of our sinful neglect, he withdraws from us so that we can't hear his voice, or see his face, or sense his love. When that happens, all our thoughts about him are barren and empty of spiritual refreshment. If we learn to be content with such lifeless thoughts of him, our spirits dry up and wither.

When we first suspect that Christ is distant, we should do what the beloved did in the Song of Songs:

On my bed by night
I sought him whom my soul loves;
    I sought him, but found him not.
I will rise now and go about the city,
    in the streets and in the squares;

> I will seek him whom my soul loves.
>> I sought him, but found him not.
> The watchmen found me
>> as they went about in the city.
> "Have you seen him whom my soul loves?"
> Scarcely had I passed them
>> when I found him whom my soul loves.
> *I held him, and would not let him go.* (Song 3:1–4; see also
>> 5:2–8)

Our glorious husband, the Lord Jesus, sometimes withdraws himself from our spiritual experience so that we have no sense of his love, no communications of his consoling grace. If we never feel his absence, it may be that we've never enjoyed his presence. But those whom he has visited with his love—whom he has refreshed, relieved, and comforted—know what it is to be left by him, even briefly. They are distressed when they look for him but can't find him.

If you find yourself in this lonesome spiritual state, turn back to the Song of Songs and learn from the beloved. Don't give up your hunt for Christ through prayer, meditation, and mourning; through reading and hearing the Word; through public and private worship; through diligent obedience—until you find him or he returns to you. And when you find him, *never let him go.*

Think of Christ as the God-Man with Appropriate Gratitude and Awe

Bathe every thought of Christ as the God-man with admiration, adoration, and gratitude. The knowledge of the God-man is an ocean whose depths we can't sound. When we're made new in Christ, our hearts and minds are enabled, by grace, to cling to him. By faith, our minds discern the nobility and beauty of Christ; by faith, our affections long for Christ; by faith, our wills embrace Christ. We learn to admire, adore, and thank him. In short, we discover what it is to obey the greatest commandment (Matt. 22:37–38).

This love that begins at our new birth should grow throughout our lives and ripen until it bears its luscious fruit in heaven, when we join our voices with the whole church of the redeemed.

> And they sang a new song, saying,
>
>> "Worthy are you to take the scroll
>>   and to open its seals,
>> for you were slain, and by your blood you ransomed people
>>   for God
>>   from every tribe and language and people and nation,
>> and you have made them a kingdom and priests to our
>>   God,
>>   and they shall reign on the earth."
>
> Then I looked, and I heard around the throne and the living creatures and the elders the voice of many angels, numbering myriads of myriads and thousands of thousands, saying with a loud voice,
>
>> "Worthy is the Lamb who was slain,
>> to receive power and wealth and wisdom and might
>> and honor and glory and blessing!"
>
> And I heard every creature in heaven and on earth and under the earth and in the sea, and all that is in them, saying,
>
>> "To him who sits on the throne and to the Lamb
>> be blessing and honor and glory and might forever and
>>   ever!"
>
> And the four living creatures said, "Amen!" and the elders fell down and worshiped. (Rev. 5:9–14)

My hope for this chapter has been to persuade you (and remind myself) that the doctrine of Christ as God and man is more than just our creed. This mystery is the glory of our Lord Jesus and is reason enough to attract us to sit beside Mary at his feet rather than be distracted with Martha (Luke 10:38–41). One glimpse of his double nature is enough to fill our hearts and minds with wonder, until we overflow with admiration, adoration, and thanksgiving—until our souls rise to an *O altitudo!*

For Reflection and Discussion

1. Christ is the Bridegroom of the church, his beautiful bride. As his bride, answer the question posed in Song of Songs 5:9: "What is your beloved more than another beloved, O most beautiful among women?"

2. Although you don't need a graduate degree in theology to meditate on Christ as God and man, you do need some basic doctrine. If you don't feel assured that the Bible teaches that Christ always has been and always will be God, that at a point in time he became a man—*and* that he continues to be both God and man forever—then before you go on, please pick one of the following resources and use it to get to know these truths from Scripture:

> The Heidelberg Catechism (with Scripture texts). Study part 2, "Man's Deliverance," questions 12–19—and make sure you look up all the Bible verses.

> Rhodes, Jonty. *Man of Sorrows, King of Glory: What the Humiliation and Exaltation of Jesus Mean for Us*. Wheaton, IL: Crossway, 2021. See esp. chap. 2, "For the Son of God, Who Came: *The Person of Christ*."

Stott, John R. W. *Basic Christianity.* London: Inter-Varsity Press, 1958. See esp. part 1, "The Person of Christ."

Calvin, John. *Institutes of the Christian Religion.* See esp. 2.12.1 through 2.14.4.

3. Identify at least three obstacles that keep you from thinking of Christ throughout the day. How does each of them crowd out thoughts of Christ? What are some things you could do to overcome these obstacles? Set aside a day of prayer (and perhaps fasting) during which you can ask God to bring these barriers down and give you delight in Christ.

4. What fills your mind throughout the day? (Work? Fantasies? Song lyrics?) Why does it fill your mind? (Necessity? Ambition? Untamed desires? Laziness? Habit?) Now, what could you learn from this that might help you to fill your mind with thoughts of Christ throughout the day?

4

he stoops down to look on the heavens

Give me the lowest place.
—Christina Rossetti

Under the Callus

If you've ever hoed a garden without work gloves, you know that rubbing the same place on your palm over and over will make a callus. And when it gets hard, you can prick a callus with a needle and feel nothing. A callus doesn't have nerve endings, so it isn't sensitive.

If you've ever belonged to a church that recites a creed week after week, you know that your mind and heart can grow callused and insensitive to the truths of our faith.[1] I confess that at times I even look around to see who has the creed memorized, my mind unmoved by the words marching out of my mouth. Still, there's a phrase in the Nicene Creed that I can hardly get past

---

1. This isn't a reason to stop saying creeds. It's a reason to seek renewed hearts.

without something catching in my throat. Speaking of Christ, we remind ourselves that

> For us and for our salvation
> *he came down* from heaven.

His love is close to the surface of this doctrine. I can't hurry past his motivation: he came down *for us*. Isn't this what grabbed Paul when he said, "I live by faith in the Son of God, who loved *me* and gave himself *for me*" (Gal. 2:20)? This is too personal to be a doctrine of the church. Doctrines are supposed to be dry as dust, right? But I marvel at what he did for us: *he came down*.

One Giant Leap for Mankind

Sin is an ocean that separates us from God. No one can swim across it. Angels with flaming swords guard the locked gate so no one can get back into the Eden of God's presence (Gen. 3:24). This is the miserable way things would have stayed, forever, if God hadn't sent a Mediator to span the ocean, unlock the gate, shatter the sword, and bring us back to him. "For there is one God, and there is one mediator between God and men, the man Christ Jesus" (1 Tim. 2:5).

Do you realize that God himself, as *God*, couldn't be the mediator between himself and us? Despite all the gracious work he did for our salvation, he couldn't in his simple divine essence be our mediator (Gal. 3:20). And of course there was no creature fit to be mediator—no creature in heaven or on earth who could fill those shoes (1 Sam. 2:25).

With no mediator in sight, the Lord Christ, the Son of God, said, "Behold, I have come to do your will, O God, as it is written of me in the scroll of the book" (Heb. 10:7). These are among the first and simplest truths of Christianity, and in these

ABCs of the faith we find a radiant display of Christ's glory. But we won't see the brightness of that glory until we consider just how far down he stepped. We have to know where he came from, as well as where he landed, in order to appreciate his giant leap for mankind.

Our Lover's Leap

My wife and I have three sons. When the oldest was fifteen, the second was six and the third five. The oldest was a bit too old to enjoy the games the little boys liked. Occasionally, though, he would build a Lego submarine or helicopter for the boys, and they would bounce and beam with delight.

Sometimes he built these toys under duress: I tried to encourage a sibling camaraderie and would, *ahem*, "ask" this kindness of him. But at unpredictable times he'd give, without prompting, one of his carefully crafted tank or fighter-plane models to his little brothers. Those moments thrilled me, because I saw in him evidence of selflessness. I knew it was hard for him to lay aside his own interests and serve them; he had nothing to gain from it.

As heartwarming as such brotherly condescension is, it can't compare to the giant leap down that our Savior took to be our Mediator. He didn't become our Mediator because the Father twisted his arm. He took the job freely (Phil. 2:5–8).

When we stop to consider how Christ came down for us, he grows more glorious in our eyes.

Just How Far Down Did Christ Come?

When the Scriptures speak of God's exaltation above his creation, they describe him as inconceivably high above us.

59

Who is like the LORD our God,
> who is seated on high,
who looks far down
> on the heavens and the earth? (Ps. 113:5–6)

Did you catch that? God has to humble himself not only to see us but even to see the *heavens*. This means he's really high above us. And he is this high above us in two ways.

God Is High above Us in His Being

No creature shares God's divine essence. In comparison to God, all nations are a drop in the bucket, "less than nothing and emptiness" (Isa. 40:17); if weighed in the scales against him, we're dust (Isa. 40:15). In fact, when we try to compare the being of God, who is the fountain of all that exists, with any of his creatures, we're left with no meaningful analogies or proportions. A molecule of water is still infinitely closer to the Pacific Ocean than the measure of our being is to God's. And it's not just that everything we say about God is understatement; he's on a different scale of being from us, another plane, absolutely beyond comparison.

So it's more than extraordinary when God draws close to his creatures. We can't fathom how low he humbles himself to do it. And when he steps down and embraces not only kings and queens, but even the dregs of society, we fall speechless before his grace. "For thus says the One who is high and lifted up, who inhabits eternity, whose name is Holy: 'I dwell in the high and holy place, and also with him who is of a contrite and lowly spirit, to revive the spirit of the lowly, and to revive the heart of the contrite'" (Isa. 57:15).

God Is High above Us in His Eternal Happiness in Himself

God doesn't need anyone or anything else in order to be happy. The Father, Son, and Holy Spirit have always been, and always will be, eternally satisfied. Within the Trinity there is perfect love. But no creature is self-sufficient. Because we are creatures, we all depend on something outside us: God.

The human nature of Christ, even in heaven, is not self-sufficient—he lives in God, and God in him; the human nature of Christ is fully dependent on God, as we are, for all good things that come from him. God alone lacks nothing, needs nothing. No one can add anything to God—"nor is he served by human hands, as though he needed anything, since he himself gives to all mankind life and breath and everything" (Acts 17:25).

Can you see how this underscores the glory of the Son of God? Think about it: If he was so infinitely and unshakably satisfied in his nature as God, what did he have to gain by taking on our frail human nature? Remember that, as God, he is so high above his creation that he must humble himself in order to regard his creatures. How much more must he have humbled himself to take on our nature in order to rescue us! It was an act without a trace of self-consideration: there was nothing for him to gain by doing it, for he already possessed all things. It was selfless, pure and simple.

Just How Did Christ Come Down?

We want to see as much of the glory of Christ, by faith, as we can. In order to see how glorious it is that he came down for us, it will help us to understand *how* he came down. Misunderstandings about this have pestered the church since the days of the apostles, so let's start by eliminating some misconceptions about what happened when the Son of God became man.[2]

---

2. I can only mention these in passing and trust you to explore them in more detail as you get to know Christ more clearly. I will suggest a few resources in the "For Reflection and Discussion" section that follows.

The Son of God Never Stopped Being God

The Scriptures clearly teach that Christ had been God from all eternity. Before time began, he was *with* God and he *was* God (John 1:1). When Paul talks about the Son coming down, he says that before he came down, he was "in very nature God"—though he "did not consider equality with God something to be used to his own advantage" (Phil. 2:6 NIV). The Son was eternally equal with God the Father. This is exactly what the unbelieving Jews accused Christ of claiming, and it was exactly what they couldn't bear (John 5:18).

Being equal with God, Christ "emptied himself, by taking the form of a servant, being born in the likeness of men" (Phil. 2:7). This is the stepping down that is so glorious: not that he ceased to be God but that, while remaining God, he took on our human nature, a nature that was light-years beneath him.[3]

The Son of God Didn't Change His Divine Nature into a Human One

Some claim that Christ turned his divine nature human, as he turned the water into wine. But where is the glory in that? If this were true, his divine nature would have been destroyed by being changed into a human nature.

The Son of God Didn't Make a New Hybrid Nature

Some suppose that Christ joined the two natures together in a mixture, like chocolate syrup and milk, to make a third nature that was neither divine nor human. Had he done this, he would have taken something away from the perfection of the divine nature. Again, what glory is there in that? There isn't the least "variation or shadow" of change in the nature of God (James 1:17).

---

3. There's much more to say about Philippians 2:6–8. See, for example, Moisés Silva, *The Wycliffe Exegetical Commentary: Philippians* (Chicago: Moody Press, 1988), 112–26.

The Son of God Hid the Glory of His Divine Nature behind His Human Nature

If Christ never ceased to be God, and he never changed the nature of God, then in what sense did he, as God, "come down"? Paul says that he "humbled himself" and "emptied himself" (Phil. 2:7–8); that is, he didn't selfishly exploit his deity. In Philippians 2:5–6, Paul teaches us not to be self-serving and shows us how Christ refused to act selfishly. In his humility, Christ didn't use his equality with God for his own advantage. He veiled the glory of his divine nature in ours so that there was no outward appearance of it. The glory of his deity was so concealed that *the world didn't even think he was a good man, much less the God of the universe.*

The Son of God Went beyond Mere Appearances

One of the first heresies that infected the church immediately after the days of the apostles was the teaching that everything Christ suffered and did as a man was in appearance only—like the angels in the Old Testament who, in the shape of men, ate and drank. That is, there was only an *appearance* of Christ in the man Jesus at Jerusalem; the Christ, they claimed, never suffered in the man Jesus. But the ancient Christians replied to these heretics, "You have found an imaginary Christ and an imaginary salvation."

The Glory of Christ's Coming Down

When Christ became man, he took our entire nature; he didn't turn it into something merely spiritual. He took real flesh and real blood, a real human heart that could grieve and break. When he suffered—when he was tried, tempted, and forsaken—he suffered just as you or I would (Heb. 4:14).

If I had an angel's pen, I could never adequately express the glory of his coming down. It is the most unutterable work of the wisdom of the Father and of the love of the Son—the boldest evidence of God's care for us. What could equal it? What can I compare to it? It's the sunshine of our religion and the life-giving soul of the gospel. It carries the mystery of the wisdom of God above our reason and understanding, past the minds of angels, until it can be only the object of faith and admiration. It's a mystery fitting the greatness of God (Job 11:7–9; Rom. 11:33–36).

He who was eternally God, who was as much a divine person as the Father and the Spirit, who has to humble himself just to look at the things in heaven and earth (Ps. 113:6), took the nature of man to be his own. From then on, he was no less man than he was God. To multiply the wonder of this mystery, he humbled himself to the point that he became a man who was despised and rejected (Isa. 53:3; John 1:11).

I'm trying to describe what's revealed in the Scriptures—what we believers hold to by faith. But when we come close to a steady, direct view of it, our minds give up. The only rest we can find is to admire and adore what we can never fully comprehend. We're at a loss, and we know that we will be as long as we're in this world.

But note this: when we're at a loss, and when we stumble into holy worship of the Son of God who came down for us, God showers his grace and benefits on us.

Here we find our sanctuary, our certain refuge. What do the distressed look for in a sanctuary? A supply to meet their needs, deliverance from all their fears, and a defense against all danger. Sin-hunted souls who flee their own guilt and God's wrath, who can't shake the shackles of sin, find their supplier, deliverer, and protector in Christ, who came down to be their sanctuary (Heb. 6:18). Do you feel the heavy load of sin on your shoulders? Are you confounded by temptation? Are you bent low under the oppression of some spiritual adversary? Gazing on the glory of Christ as he came down *for you* can support and relieve you.

Any time we look for people to help us, we need to know two things: Are they *willing* to help us? Are they *able* to help us? One without the other might be impressive or sweet, but it won't bring relief. But we find both in Christ. What will he not do for us? He emptied and humbled himself—stepped infinitely down from the prerogative of the glory that was his because of his being and self-sufficiency. Won't he relieve us from all our distress? Won't he do for us everything we need? Won't he be a sanctuary for us?

And we have no reason to doubt his power to help us, because by coming down to be a suffering man, Jesus gave up nothing of his power as God, nothing of his wisdom or grace. He could still do everything that he could always do, as God, from eternity. So as we see his glory as the one who came down for us, we worship him; we find our sanctuary; we "rejoice with joy that is inexpressible and filled with glory" (1 Peter 1:8).

The next time you find yourself in church yawning through the creed, stop. Think about the words. Think about what it means that

> for us and for our salvation
> *he came down.*

For Reflection and Discussion

1. Christ is the Bridegroom of the church, his beautiful bride. With this in mind, answer the question that is posed in Song of Songs 5:9: "What is your beloved more than another beloved, O most beautiful among women?"

2. Why is it important to know that Christ has always been God and has never stopped being God?

3. Why is it important to know that Christ became a man—a real human man?

4. In this chapter, we learned of the benefit of reflecting on the fact that Christ came down for us: namely, we find our sanctuary in him. Can you think of any other benefits that might grow out of such meditation? After you've tried to think of some, read what Paul says in 2 Corinthians 5:14, looking at the surrounding verses for context. Does that suggest another benefit to you?

5. Because there are many misunderstandings about Christ's person, and because we want to worship him in spirit and in truth as he has revealed himself, we benefit from knowing and understanding teachings about Christ that the church has rejected. The following resources may challenge you, but they will be worth the effort:

> Wellum, Stephen J. *The Person of Christ: An Introduction.* Short Studies in Systematic Theology, edited by Graham A. Cole and Oren R. Martin. Wheaton, IL: Crossway, 2021. Wellum includes a helpful glossary in the back, as well as a trove of good recommendations for further reading.

> Brown, Harold O. J. *Heresies: The Image of Christ in the Mirror of Heresy and Orthodoxy from the Apostles to the Present.* Grand Rapids: Baker, 1988.

> Martin, Walter, with Jill Martin Rische. *The Kingdom of the Cults Handbook: Quick Reference Guide to Alternative Belief Systems.* Minneapolis, MN: Bethany House, 2019.

6. This is another ambitious project, but it could benefit you. Choose a modern religion that is a heretical sect of Christianity,

such as the Church of Jesus Christ of Latter-day Saints (Mormonism) or the Jehovah's Witnesses. Find out what it teaches about Christ—whether it says he is God and man or something else. If it teaches that he is anything other than God and man, describe how it robs him of his glory.

His Saviour's Words, Going to the Cross

Have, have ye no regard, all ye
Who pass this way, to pity me,
Who am a man of misery!

A man both bruised, and broke, and one
Who suffers not here for mine own,
But for my friends' transgression!

Ah! Sion's Daughters, do not fear
The Crosse, the Cords, the Nails, the Spear,
The Myrrh, the Gall, the Vinegar:

For Christ, your loving Saviour, hath
Drunk up the wine of Gods fierce wrath;
Only, there's left a little froth,

Less for to taste, than for to shew,
What bitter cups had been your due,
Had He not drank them up for you.

ROBERT HERRICK

5

the river of love

> *It is unbought love. . . . You have no cause to boast. He loved*
> *you, because he loved you—for nothing. O what a black soul*
> *wast thou, when Christ set his love upon thee!*
> —ROBERT MURRAY M'CHEYNE

Cur Deus Homo

In the eleventh century, Anselm sat down to explain *Cur Deus Homo*—"Why God Became Man." He wrote for the sake of his brothers and sisters, "that they may be gladdened by understanding and meditating on those things that they believe." His book is now a jewel in the treasury of the church. He masterfully demonstrated how no being except the God-man could atone for our sins and save us.

Anselm showed that the Son of God became man because there was no other way to save us. But if we were to ask Christ why he became man—not why he *needed* to become man, but why he *wanted* to—his answer could be summed up in one word: love.

The life I now live in the flesh I live by faith in the Son of God, who loved me and gave himself for me. (Gal. 2:20)

By this we know love, that he laid down his life for us. (1 John 3:16)

To him who loves us and has freed us from our sins by his blood and made us a kingdom, priests to his God and Father, to him be glory and dominion forever and ever. Amen. (Rev. 1:5–6)

When we gaze on the glory of Christ, it's difficult for us to escape his love. But before we dip our cupped hands into the refreshing river of Christ's love in all its glory, let's step upstream and see its headwaters.

The Fountain of Love in Eternity

Christ's love for us springs from the Father's eternal love for us. Again and again, the Bible returns us to this fountain of love, which is the sure source of all our hope and joy. The Father's love is eternally expressed in what he determined to do "before the foundation of the world" (Eph. 1:4) and in how he carried it out by sending his Son (John 3:16). We see the inexpressible love of the God who determines to draw us close to himself through the blood of the Son and the sanctification of the Spirit.

But we ought always to give thanks to God for you, brothers beloved by the Lord, because God chose you as the firstfruits to be saved, through sanctification by the Spirit and belief in the truth. (2 Thess. 2:13)

To those who are elect . . . according to the foreknowledge of God the Father, in the sanctification of the Spirit, for obedience to Jesus Christ and for sprinkling with his blood. (1 Peter 1:1–2)

The Father's determination to rescue us is called love not because he loves us "just the way we are." He loves us so much that he *can't* leave us the way we are—his plan includes changing us and making us into new creatures who are pleasing to him. No, the Father's determination to save us is called love for the following reasons.

The Father's Determination to Save Us Flows from His Very Nature as Love

"God is love" (1 John 4:8; see also v. 9). Only God's own essence could have caused him to choose us by an eternal act of his will, because in eternity nothing else existed that could have caused his love. And although his determination to save us expresses all his perfections, it most explicitly expresses his love. Yes, his saving us expresses his righteousness, holiness, wisdom, goodness, truth—everything that he is. But it especially declares that God is love.

The Father's Determination to Save Us Was Free and Undeserved

He chose to love us in eternity, long before we appeared in history. He chose us before there was anything good in us that could have excited his love (Rom. 9:11). Since we had no way to win his love, the cause behind his choosing us must have come from within him, not from us. In fact, whatever in us is lovable is a result of his work to save us—"even as he chose us in him before the foundation of the world, that we should be holy and blameless before him" (Eph. 1:4).

The Father's Determination to Save Us Set Off a Chain Reaction of Love

God saves us through multiplied acts of love. Let's slow down and consider the chain of the actions he performed on

our behalf to save us. Think of his choice, in eternity, to save us.
Think of the mystery of his wise plan to save us through his Son.
Think of his preparations to save us, all the groundwork he laid
through Israel and the covenants. Think of his willingness to turn
his back on his beloved Son, in whom he was well pleased—for
our sake. Think of the power he displayed by raising Christ from
the dead and seating him at his right hand to pray for us so that
we will endure to the end.

> For God so loved the world, that he gave his only Son, that
> whoever believes in him should not perish but have eternal
> life. (John 3:16)

> I have loved you with an everlasting love;
>> therefore I have continued my faithfulness to you.
>> (Jer. 31:3)

> Blessed be the God and Father of our Lord Jesus Christ,
> who has blessed us in Christ with every spiritual blessing
> in the heavenly places, even as he chose us in him before
> the foundation of the world, that we should be holy and
> blameless before him. In love he predestined us for adoption
> to himself as sons through Jesus Christ, according to the
> purpose of his will. (Eph. 1:3–5)

> Anyone who does not love does not know God, because God
> is love. In this the love of God was made manifest among us,
> that God sent his only Son into the world, so that we might
> live through him. . . .
>
> So we have come to know and to believe the love that
> God has for us. God is love, and whoever abides in love
> abides in God, and God abides in him. (1 John 4:8–9, 16)

Let's not stop with thoughts of the Father's love as it unfolds in Scripture; reflect on your own story and how his chain of loving acts extends through your life. Did he show his love to you by bringing you into the world in a Christian home? Did he send a friend into your life at just the right time to bring you to Jesus? Did he reach down to you when you were on the brink of taking your own life? Our testimonies to his grace in our lives are offerings of praise to him, a way in which we see his glory.

The River of Love throughout History

Thoughts of the Father's plan to save us are enough to overwhelm our hearts day after day. But our goal is to reflect on the glory of Christ, and it is glorious that the Father worked all his plans of love through Christ. The Father's love is the fountain, and it flows to us only through Christ. We would never know the Father's love except through him.

To reflect on Christ's love, let's trace the path the river of love takes throughout history.

At first, people were made in God's image and therefore loved him and were loved by him. All that they were, had, or hoped for sprang from his goodness and love. Every breath they took was one of love for God. It was paradise on earth—preparation for an eternal life of love in heaven.

By their sin, they tumbled out of this paradise of love. With a taste of forbidden fruit, they changed from God's lovers to his enemies. They brought on themselves, and on us, every misery: sorrows in this life as well as the threat of unending miseries in hell.

While we were in such a wretched state, Christ's first act of love toward us was born of pity and compassion. The Scriptures celebrate how our divine Knight hears our cries—the cries of his damsel in distress—and is moved.

Since therefore the children share in flesh and blood, he himself likewise partook of the same things, that through death he might destroy the one who has the power of death, that is, the devil, and deliver all those who through fear of death were subject to lifelong slavery. (Heb. 2:14–15)

In all their affliction *he was afflicted*,
    and the angel of his presence saved them;
in his love and in his pity he redeemed them. (Isa. 63:9)

Once we had become the apple of his eye, Christ took up his work for us with inexplicable delight (Prov. 8:30–31). Where did this compassion and joy come from? What drove him who was eternally blessed to concern himself with such helpless, miserable creatures? "He saved us, not because of works done by us in righteousness, but according to his own mercy" (Titus 3:5).

The Son, eager to save his people, hears (as it were) from the Father the way he can save mankind. The road leads through the darkest difficulties. Of course, no obstacles could slow the Son *as God*, yet this plan would be hard because it demanded that he carry it out in human nature. The plan required the Son to pity us until there was no one left to pity him—to chase his delight to save us until his soul was crushed under sorrow, to relieve our sufferings by suffering what we should have suffered.

But none of this deterred Christ from taking up this work of love and mercy for us. On the contrary, his love rose to this plan like waves that are driven before a hurricane. He heard this plan and said, "Behold, I have come to do your will, O God, as it is written of me in the scroll of the book" (Heb. 10:7; see also Isa. 50:5–7).

So the Father prepared a body for him. In his human nature, body and soul, he would carry out his mission of love. The Father gave him his human nature just for this and filled him with immeasurable grace.

Can you see that this glorious love of Christ isn't only the love of a divine person? The Father's love is the love of God. Although this may sound strange, there's something more in the love of Christ. When he loved us, he was God *and* man. As a man, he shattered every obstacle and loved us to the fullest: he died for us. This is something that God as God couldn't do.

Now, when we talk about Christ's loving us, we can talk about how he loves us as God and how he loves us as man—we can distinguish human acts from those that are divine. For example, it was an act of inexpressible love to take on our nature (Heb. 2:14, 17). Christ did this in his *divine* nature, because he did it before he became man. It was another act of his inconceivable love to lay down his life for us (1 John 3:16), yet this was an act of his *human* nature. But in every act we consider we are still looking at the love of one person: Jesus Christ. This one person is the God-man, so we can say with the Scriptures that *God* laid down his life for us and purchased the church with his own blood (Acts 20:28).

This love is the glory of Christ. It soars over our heads, beyond the reach of our understanding. But we can adore it by faith.

Fixing His Love in Our Hearts

Even what we can comprehend of Christ's love is marvelous. I hope to stir your heart—and mine—to steadily and patiently reflect on this love.

Work to Ready Your Mind for Heavenly Thoughts

If our thoughts are prisoners of our flesh or can't rise above our earthly needs, we won't be able to hold on to a sense of Christ's love and its glory. High thoughts of his love can't live in the same mind with earthbound thoughts any more than a mouse can live in the same cage with a boa constrictor. Just as the serpent devours the rodent, a mind charmed by worldliness eats up the first feeble attempt to gaze on the Son. So we "seek the things that are above, where Christ is, seated at the right hand of God" and set our "minds on things that are above, not on things that are on earth" (Col. 3:1–2).[1]

Don't Be Satisfied with Vague Meditations about the Love of Christ

Generic ideas of love won't display Christ's glory to our minds. Knowing that Italy is a boot-shaped country in southern Europe doesn't move us, but when we walk the ancient narrow streets of Florence past Dante's house, taste the silky gelato handed to us by a laughing vendor, stretch out on the grassy slopes of the Boboli Gardens of the Palazzo Pitti, and climb the steps of the Duomo to watch the sun set over the red-gold ribbon of the Arno—then our hearts sing *la gloria d'Italia*!

Relish Christ's love in fine detail: Remember that it's the Lord of glory himself, the Son of God, who loves you. Remember that he loved you so much that he gladly died for you. As you read his Word, mark the ways he has loved you, *as God*, through acts of wisdom, goodness, and grace; note the pity and compassion he had for you *as a man*—how his human heart was warm toward you (Eph. 3:19; Heb. 2:14–15). Let your mind linger over how free his love is, how it is not compelled by anything outside him, and how completely you don't deserve his love (1 John 4:10). In fact, think about what you truly deserved from him, and let

1. For a thorough treatment of setting our minds on things above, see John Owen, *The Grace and Duty of Being Spiritually Minded*, reprinted in *The Works of John Owen*, ed. William H. Goold, vol. 7 (Edinburgh: Johnstone & Hunter, 1852; repr., Banner of Truth Trust, 1991), 262–497. I've also adapted Owen's work in *The Devoted Mind: Seeking God's Face in a World of Distraction* (Phillipsburg, NJ: P&R Publishing, 2023).

that melt your heart before him. Then turn these details back to him in praise.

Don't Be Content to Be Correct

Right thoughts about Christ's love are lifeless when our hearts aren't moved toward him. If your mind reflects on him but your heart is cold, any sweet thoughts you've mustered will fade faster than clouds in your coffee. But Christ is meat for our souls. Nothing in him nourishes our hearts more than his love; we should always hunger for it.

The love of Christ is glorious. No creature, angelic or human, could ever have dreamed the least of this love before the Lamb of God came into the world to show it. And now that he has come, his love towers above our highest and best thoughts, until we gasp in wonder.

For Reflection and Discussion

1. Christ is the Bridegroom of the church, his beautiful bride. With this in mind, answer the question that is posed in Song of Songs 5:9: "What is your beloved more than another beloved, O most beautiful among women?"

2. How is it glorious that Christ alone reveals the Father's love?

3. What do you think of the statement that the Son's love is somehow more than "mere" divine love, because he is both God and man?

4. Write a prayer of praise that tells the story of how God saved you. Trace his acts of love in your life that brought you to faith. Be detailed and specific.

5. Make a list of the difficulties and hardships that Jesus had to overcome in his human nature to carry out his mission of love for you. Again, be specific. How does reading through this list make you feel about Christ?

6

a hero to worship

See, the conquering hero comes!
Sound the trumpets, beat the drums!
—THOMAS MORELL

What Makes a Hero Glorious?

What makes a hero shine in your eyes? Is it the quiet courage and loyalty of Sam Gamgee, who stuck to Frodo's side all the way to Mount Doom? The nobility of Shakespeare's Henry V, who inspired his badly outnumbered troops before the battle of Agincourt? Or perhaps the unrelenting love of Jean Valjean, who bore the unconscious body of Marius through the sewers of Paris to safety?

Whatever heroic traits come to your mind, I suspect that *obedience* and *suffering* aren't among them. Yet it's because of his obedience to God's law, and his suffering of the curse of that law for us, that Christ is our Conquering Hero.

A hidden glory surrounded Christ as he obeyed and suffered. If the rulers of the world had seen it, they wouldn't have crucified the Lord of glory (1 Cor. 2:8). Yet some saw this glory. They saw "his glory, glory as of the only Son from the Father" (John 1:14), and they saw it when others saw no beauty or majesty in him, "nothing in his appearance" that anyone could desire (Isa. 53:2 NIV). It's the same today. Those who see his glory see it by faith. So, by faith, let's draw back the curtain on the drama of Christ's glory to witness his heroic obedience and suffering for us.

Our Hero Conquered by Obedience

In our society, we expect a hero to bend the rules and defy authority to save the world. But our hero saved us by *obeying*. If we look closely at the nature of Christ's obedience, we'll see its glory.

His Obedience Was Free

Think about what it means for us to obey God. Because we're creatures, we're obliged to obey our Creator. We aren't autonomous; no matter how much our flesh would like to live outside God's law, we can't. But since we are under this obligation, our obedience can be beautiful when we obey freely, and from the heart, without having to be led by bit and bridle like a stubborn mule (Ps. 32:9). The child who says "I'm sorry" to her brother only because her father is standing over her looking stern is not obeying from the heart. There's no glory in performing obedience under duress.

The situation was different for the Son of God; it made his obedience more beautiful than any obedience of ours. In the beginning, before he became a man, he wasn't a creature, so he wasn't naturally subject to the law. In fact, he was the Lord of the law. But he freely chose to subject himself to the law when he said, "Behold, I have come to do your will, O God, as it is written of me in the scroll of the book" (Heb. 10:7). Christ obeyed because he wanted to.

His choice was just the beginning of the glory of his obedience. The wisdom, grace, love, and humility of this choice animated every act of his obedience, making it pleasing to God and redemptive to us. Christ set out to fulfill the law for others, since he had no need to fulfill it for himself. When he asked John to baptize him, John refused at first because he knew Jesus had nothing to repent of, but Jesus said, "Let it be so now, for thus it is fitting for us to fulfill all righteousness" (Matt. 3:15). The fact that the one who was Lord of the universe submitted himself to careful, thorough obedience savors of his glorious grace.

His Obedience Wasn't for Him but for Us

We were obliged to obey and couldn't; he wasn't obliged to obey (except by his choice) and did. God gave him the honor of obeying for his people, "so by the one man's obedience the many will be made righteous" (Rom. 5:19). That the perfect obedience of one man can save the entire church is glorious.

His Obedience Perfectly and Fully Represented the Holiness of God

The glory of God's holiness was seen in the law when he wrote the Ten Commandments with his finger on the stone tablets, and it is even more brilliantly displayed when he writes his law on the hearts of believers. But the only complete and perfect example of God's holiness that we have is the holiness and obedience of Christ, who answered God's commands in every detail.

He Obeyed in the Face of Extreme Obstacles and Opposition

Although he was free from the sinful flesh that remains in Christians and makes perfect obedience impossible for us, Christ met more external opposition in the form of temptation, suffering, attacks, and denials than we will ever meet. So the Father says of him, "Although he was a son, he learned obedience through what he suffered" (Heb. 5:8). He didn't learn *how* to obey; he learned *what it cost* to obey. He resisted temptation to the point of shedding his blood: we see he would rather die than break the least of God's commands (Heb. 12:1–4).

His Obedience Shines Brightest When We Think about Who He Is

None other than the Son of God—he who was in heaven, above all and Lord of all—lived in the world as a person of no reputation and walked a path of the strictest obedience to the whole law of God. Godly people prayed to him, yet he himself prayed night and day. All the angels of heaven and all creatures worshiped him, yet he continually carried out all the duties of the worship of God.

He was Lord over the house, yet he diligently observed the office of the lowest servant in the house. He made all people and held them in his hand as a potter holds clay, yet he lived among them as a man and gave all people their due—and, beyond that, he showed mercy and kindness to them and gave them good things that weren't deserved. The obedience of Christ is both mysterious and glorious in our eyes.

Our Hero Conquered by Suffering

The prophets often describe Christ's work in terms of victory, success, and glorious triumph.

> Who is this who comes from Edom,
>   in crimsoned garments from Bozrah,
> he who is splendid in his apparel,
>   marching in the greatness of his strength?
> "It is I, speaking in righteousness,
>   mighty to save."

Why is your apparel red,
and your garments like his who treads in the winepress?

"I have trodden the winepress alone,
and from the peoples no one was with me;
I trod them in my anger
and trampled them in my wrath;
their lifeblood spattered on my garments,
and stained all my apparel.
For the day of vengeance was in my heart,
and my year of redemption had come.
I looked, but there was no one to help;
I was appalled, but there was no one to uphold;
so my own arm brought me salvation,
and my wrath upheld me." (Isa. 63:1–5)

But before he was exalted in triumph he had to suffer, as he explained to his disciples on the road to Emmaus: "Was it not necessary that the Christ should suffer these things and enter into his glory?" (Luke 24:26; see also Matt. 16:21; Mark 8:31; Luke 9:22; 17:25). Some of these sufferings came immediately from God above; others from devils and wicked people who were acting according to God's wise plan.

When we begin to consider his sufferings, our minds recoil; we can't conceive how much he must have endured. We can't launch into this ocean in meditation without quickly feeling unable to plumb its depths. In this chapter, I'll only begin to point toward the glory of our Lord's sufferings; the greater part of them will stay behind the veil.

Think of your Lord Jesus as he was crushed under the full weight of God's wrath—under the curse of the law. Think of him as he took on the worst with which God had ever threatened sin or sinners. Think of him as he agonized in bloody sweat in the garden of Gethsemane—of his loud cries and prayers as he sorrowed to the point of death, amazed at the things that were coming on him (Matt. 26:36–46; Mark 14:32–42; Luke 22:39–48). Think of him as he battled against all the powers of darkness—against the rage and madness of men. Think of him as he suffered in body and soul. Think of him as he lost his name, his reputation, his goods, his life. Think of him as he prayed, wept, cried out, bled, died—and in all this making his soul an offering for sin.

> By oppression and judgment he was taken away;
>> and as for his generation, who considered
> that he was cut off out of the land of the living,
>> stricken for the transgression of my people? (Isa. 53:8)

Explore Christ's sufferings for you until you're overwhelmed with holy admiration.

> What is man that you are mindful of him,
>> and the son of man that you care for him? (Ps. 8:4)

> Who has measured the Spirit of the LORD,
>> or what man shows him his counsel? (Isa. 40:13)

> Oh, the depth of the riches and wisdom and knowledge of God! How unsearchable are his judgments and how inscrutable his ways! (Rom. 11:33)

What can we say in response to this? God didn't withhold his only Son but gave him up to death and to these evils for us poor, lost sinners. For our sakes, the eternal Son of God submitted himself to all the misery that our sins deserved so that we might be delivered from it completely.

The suffering Lamb is glorious in our eyes.

When Adam sinned and eternally ruined himself and all his descendants, he stood ashamed and trembling, ready to perish forever, under the frown of God. He deserved death, and he expected to be executed on the spot. Yet God promised him the gospel (Gen. 3:15). It is as if the Lord Jesus came to him and said, "Poor creature! How wretched you have become! What happened to the beauty and glory of that image of God in which you were made? How is it that you've taken the monstrous image of Satan? And yet your present misery is nothing compared with what's to come—eternal torment lies before you.

"But look up once more; look to me, that you may have some glimpse of the designs of infinite wisdom, love, and grace. Come out of your childish hiding place. I'll put myself in your plight. I'll bear the burden of guilt and the punishment that would sink you into hell. I'll repay that which I never took, and be made a curse for you, that you might be blessed forever."

He says the same to us sinners; he invites us to come to him.

Adoring the Slain Lamb

Before our very eyes, Jesus Christ has been clearly portrayed as crucified (Gal. 3:1). So let's gaze in wonder as he is poor, despised, persecuted, reproached, reviled, and hanged on a tree. And remember that while he's facing such an onslaught from the outside, he also knows and feels in his soul the full wrath of God against our sins.

But why is his misery recorded for us so clearly in the gospel and so often preached to us from the pulpit? What glory is there in such suffering? Aren't these the very things that Jews and Greeks stumbled over and took offense at (1 Cor. 1:23)? Doesn't the world think we're fools to look for help from the miseries of Christ? To look for life through his death?

Such is the wisdom of the world. But to us who believe, the sufferings of our Lord are honorable, glorious, and precious. We see in them the wisdom and power of God.

For it stands in Scripture:

> "Behold, I am laying in Zion a stone,
>   a cornerstone chosen and precious,
> and whoever believes in him will not be put to shame."

So the honor is for you who believe, but for those who do not believe,

> "The stone that the builders rejected
>   has become the cornerstone,"

and

> "A stone of stumbling,
>   and a rock of offense."

They stumble because they disobey the word, as they were destined to do.

But you are a chosen race, a royal priesthood, a holy nation, a people for his own possession, that you may proclaim the excellencies of him who called you out of darkness into his marvelous light. (1 Peter 2:6–9)

We preach Christ crucified, a stumbling block to Jews and folly to Gentiles, but to those who are called, both Jews and Greeks, Christ the power of God and the wisdom of God. For the foolishness of God is wiser than men, and the weakness of God is stronger than men. (1 Cor. 1:23–25)

God has made his light shine in the darkness of our hearts and has opened our eyes to see his wisdom and power displayed in Christ *crucified*. So we have new eyes—eyes of faith that can look at Christ beaten and bleeding and can see our Hero. By faith, we know that by those bloody stripes we're healed (Isa. 53:5; 1 Peter 2:24). And by faith we enter heaven and join one another around the throne of the slain Lamb.

> And between the throne and the four living creatures and among the elders I saw a Lamb standing, as though it had been slain, with seven horns and with seven eyes, which are the seven spirits of God sent out into all the earth. And he went and took the scroll from the right hand of him who was seated on the throne. And when he had taken the scroll, the four living creatures and the twenty-four elders fell down before the Lamb, each holding a harp, and golden bowls full of incense, which are the prayers of the saints. And they sang a new song, saying,
>
> > "Worthy are you to take the scroll
> >   and to open its seals,
> > for you were slain, and by your blood you ransomed people
> >   for God
> >   from every tribe and language and people and nation,
> > and you have made them a kingdom and priests to our God,
> >   and they shall reign on the earth."
>
> Then I looked, and I heard around the throne and the living creatures and the elders the voice of many angels, numbering myriads of myriads and thousands of thousands, saying with a loud voice,
>
> > "Worthy is the Lamb who was slain,
> > to receive power and wealth and wisdom and might
> > and honor and glory and blessing!"

And I heard every creature in heaven and on earth and under the earth and in the sea, and all that is in them, saying,

> "To him who sits on the throne and to the Lamb
> be blessing and honor and glory and might forever and
> ever!"

And the four living creatures said, "Amen!" and the elders fell down and worshiped. (Rev. 5:6–14)

For Reflection and Discussion

1. Christ is the Bridegroom of the church, his beautiful bride. With this in mind, answer the question that is posed in Song of Songs 5:9: "What is your beloved more than another beloved, O most beautiful among women?"

2. How do you define *heroic*?

3. What is heroic about Christ's obedience?

4. What is heroic about Christ's suffering?

5. Choose a passage of Scripture that speaks of the sufferings of our Lord (such as Isa. 52:13–53:12; Matt. 26:36–46; or Matt. 27:27–56). After meditating on these verses, write a brief prayer of praise to Christ for enduring these sufferings. Use details from the Scripture passage to make your prayer specific: tell him exactly what you admire about him.

6. George Herbert wrote a poem in 1633 called "The Sacrifice" that meditates at length on Christ's suffering. In the poem, Christ speaks; Herbert relates through his eyes many things that broke

his heart in the days leading up to and including his crucifixion. I've included the poem after this chapter; its spelling and capitalization are modernized. Set aside a day or two of your private prayers to work through its stanzas before Christ as you adore him for all that he suffered for you.

The Sacrifice

O, all ye, who pass by, whose eyes and mind
To worldly things are sharp, but to me blind;
To me, who took eyes that I might you find:
                    Was ever grief like mine?

The Princes of my people make a head
Against their Maker: they do wish me dead,
Who cannot wish, except I give them bread:
                    Was ever grief like mine?

Without me each one, who doth now me brave,
Had to this day been an Egyptian slave.
They use that power against me, which I gave:
                    Was ever grief like mine?

Mine own Apostle, who the bag did bear,
Though he had all I had, did not forbear
To sell me also, and to put me there:
                    Was ever grief like mine?

For thirty pence he did my death devise,
Who at three hundred did the ointment prize,
Not half so sweet as my sweet sacrifice:
                    Was ever grief like mine?

Therefore my soul melts, and my heart's dear treasure
Drops blood (the only beads) my words to measure:
O let this cup pass, if it be thy pleasure:
                    Was ever grief like mine?

These drops being tempered with a sinner's tears,
A Balsam are for both the Hemispheres:
Curing all wounds, but mine; all, but my fears:
                    Was ever grief like mine?

Yet my Disciples sleep: I cannot gain
One hour of watching; but their drowsy brain
Comforts not me, and doth my doctrine stain:
                    Was ever grief like mine?

Arise, arise, they come. Look how they run.
Alas! what haste they make to be undone!
How with their lanterns do they seek the sun!
                    Was ever grief like mine?

With clubs and staves they seek me, as a thief,
Who am the way of truth, the true relief;
Most true to those, who are my greatest grief:
                    Was ever grief like mine?

Judas, dost thou betray me with a kiss?
Canst thou find hell about my lips? and miss
Of life, just at the gates of life and bliss?
                    Was ever grief like mine?

See, they lay hold on me, not with the hands
Of faith, but fury: yet at their commands
I suffer binding, who have loosed their bands:
                    Was ever grief like mine?

All my Disciples fly; fear puts a bar
Betwixt my friends and me. They leave the star,
That brought the wise men of the East from far.
                    Was ever grief like mine?

Then from one ruler to another bound
They lead me; urging, that it was not sound
What I taught: Comments would the text confound.
                    Was ever grief like mine?

The Priest and rulers all false witness seek
'Gainst him, who seeks not life, but is the meek
And ready Paschal Lamb of this great week:
                    Was ever grief like mine?

Then they accuse me of great blasphemy,
That I did thrust into the Deity,
Who never thought that any robbery:
                    Was ever grief like mine?

Some said, that I the Temple to the floor
In three days razed, and raisèd as before.
Why, he that built the world can do much more:
                    Was ever grief like mine?

Then they condemn me all with that same breath,
Which I do give them daily, unto death.
Thus *Adam* my first breathing rendereth:
                    Was ever grief like mine?

They bind, and lead me unto *Herod*: he
Sends me to *Pilate*. This makes them agree;
But yet their friendship is my enmity:
                      Was ever grief like mine?

Herod and all his bands do set me light,
Who teach all hands to war, fingers to fight,
And only am the Lord of hosts and might:
                      Was ever grief like mine?

Herod in judgement sits, while I do stand;
Examines me with a censorious hand:
I him obey, who all things else command:
                      Was ever grief like mine?

The *Jews* accuse me with despitefulness;
And vying malice with my gentleness,
Pick quarrels with their only happiness:
                      Was ever grief like mine?

I answer nothing, but with patience prove
If stony hearts will melt with gentle love.
But who does hawk at eagles with a dove?
                      Was ever grief like mine?

My silence rather doth augment their cry;
My dove doth back into my bosom fly,
Because the raging waters still are high:
                      Was ever grief like mine?

Hark how they cry aloud still, *Crucify:*
It is not fit he live a day, they cry,
Who cannot live less than eternally:
                              Was ever grief like mine?

Pilate a stranger holdeth off; but they,
Mine own dear people, cry, *Away, away,*
With noises confused frighting the day:
                              Was ever grief like mine?

Yet still they shout, and cry, and stop their ears,
Putting my life among their sins and fears,
And therefore wish *my blood on them and theirs*:
                              Was ever grief like mine?

See how spite cankers things. These words aright
Uséd, and wishèd, are the whole world's light:
But honey is their gall, brightness their night:
                              Was ever grief like mine?

They choose a murderer, and all agree
In him to do themselves a courtesy:
For it was their own cause who killed me:
                              Was ever grief like mine?

And a seditious murderer he was:
But I the Prince of peace; peace that doth pass
All understanding, more than heav'n doth glass:
                              Was ever grief like mine?

Why, Caesar is their only King, not I:
He clave the stony rock, when they were dry;
But surely not their hearts, as I well try:
                              Was ever grief like mine?

Ah! how they scourge me! yet my tenderness
Doubles each lash: and yet their bitterness
Winds up my grief to a mysteriousness:
                              Was ever grief like mine?

They buffet me, and box me as they list,
Who grasp the earth and heaven with my fist,
And never yet, whom I would punish, missed:
                              Was ever grief like mine?

Behold, they spit on me in scornful wise,
Who by my spittle gave the blind man eyes,
Leaving his blindness to mine enemies:
                              Was ever grief like mine?

My face they cover, though it be divine.
As *Moses'* face was veilèd, so is mine,
Lest on their double-dark souls either shine:
                              Was ever grief like mine?

Servants and abjects flout me; they are witty:
Now prophesy who strikes thee, is their ditty.
So they in me deny themselves all pity:
                              Was ever grief like mine?

And now I am delivered unto death,
Which each one calls for so with utmost breath,
That he before me well nigh suffereth:
                    Was ever grief like mine?

Weep not, dear friends, since I for both have wept
When all my tears were blood, the while you slept:
Your tears for your own fortunes should be kept:
                    Was ever grief like mine?

The soldiers lead me to the common hall;
There they deride me, they abuse me all:
Yet for twelve heav'nly legions I could call:
                    Was ever grief like mine?

Then with a scarlet robe they me array;
Which shows my blood to be the only way,
And cordial left to repair man's decay:
                    Was ever grief like mine?

Then on my head a crown of thorns I wear:
For these are all the grapes *Sion* doth bear,
Though I my vine planted and watered there:
                    Was ever grief like mine?

So sits the earth's great curse in *Adam's* fall
Upon my head: so I remove it all
From th' earth unto my brows, and bear the thrall;
                    Was ever grief like mine?

Then with the reed they gave to me before,
They strike my head, the rock from whence all store
Of heav'nly blessings issue evermore:
                        Was ever grief like mine?

They bow their knees to me, and cry, *Hail king*:
Whatever scoffs or scornfulness can bring,
I am the floor, the sink, where they it fling:
                        Was ever grief like mine?

Yet since man's sceptres are as frail as reeds,
And thorny all their crowns, bloody their weeds;
I, who am Truth, turn into truth their deeds:
                        Was ever grief like mine?

The soldiers also spit upon that face,
Which Angels did desire to have the grace
And Prophets once to see, but found no place:
                        Was ever grief like mine?

Thus trimmèd forth they bring me to the rout,
Who *Crucify him*, cry with one strong shout.
God holds his peace at man, and man cries out:
                        Was ever grief like mine?

They lead me in once more, and putting then
Mine own clothes on, they lead me out again.
Whom devils fly, thus is he tossed of men:
                        Was ever grief like mine?

And now weary of sport, glad to engross
All spite in one, counting my life their loss,
They carry me to my most bitter cross:
                    Was ever grief like mine?

My cross I bear myself, until I faint:
Then Simon bears it for me by constraint,
The decreed burden of each mortal Saint:
                    Was ever grief like mine?

O all ye who pass by, behold and see;
Man stole the fruit, but I must climb the tree;
The tree of life to all, but only me:
                    Was ever grief like mine?

Lo, here I hang, charged with a world of sin,
The greater world o' th' two; for that came in
By words, but this by sorrow I must win:
                    Was ever grief like mine?

Such sorrow, as if sinful man could feel,
Or feel his part, he would not cease to kneel
Till all were melted, though he were all steel:
                    Was ever grief like mine?

But, *O my God, my God!* why leav'st thou me,
The son, in whom thou dost delight to be?
My God, my God————
                    Never was grief like mine.

Shame tears my soul, my body many a wound;
Sharp nails pierce this, but sharper that confound;
Reproaches, which are free, while I am bound.
                    Was ever grief like mine?

Now heal thyself, Physician; now come down.
Alas! I did so, when I left my crown
And father's smile for you, to feel his frown:
                    Was ever grief like mine?

In healing not myself, there doth consist
All that salvation, which ye now resist;
Your safety in my sickness doth subsist:
                    Was ever grief like mine?

Betwixt two thieves I spend my utmost breath,
As he that for some robbery suffereth.
Alas! what have I stolen from you? death:
                    Was ever grief like mine?

A king my title is, prefixed on high;
Yet by my subjects am condemned to die
A servile death in servile company:
                    Was ever grief like mine?

They gave me vinegar mingled with gall,
But more with malice: yet, when they did call,
With Manna, Angel's food, I fed them all:
                    Was ever grief like mine?

They part my garments, and by lot dispose
My coat, the type of love, which once cured those
Who sought for help, never malicious foes:
                              Was ever grief like mine?

Nay, after death their spite shall further go;
For they will pierce my side, I full well know;
That as sin came, so Sacraments might flow:
                              Was ever grief like mine?

But now I die; now all is finishèd.
My woe, man's weal: and now I bow my head.
Only let others say, when I am dead,
                              Never was grief like mine.

GEORGE HERBERT

7

God's right-hand man

. . . Every wretch, pining and pale before,
Beholding him, plucks comfort from his looks.
—William Shakespeare

A King in a Cloak

It's 3:00 in the morning before the Battle of Agincourt. The campfires of the French and the English can be seen burning in the night, and the sounds of hammers on armor "give dreadful note of preparation." The cocky French crow like roosters, while the heavily outnumbered English stare at the moon like "so many horrid ghosts."[1]

In Shakespeare's version of the history of Henry V, the king takes the cloak of Sir Thomas Erpingham and walks among his men. No one recognizes King Henry in the darkness and under the hood of his cloak. This changes the tone of his conversations. One takes place around a fire with John Bates, Alexander Court, and Michael Williams; they're arguing whether their conflict with the French is just and what moral responsibility the soldiers have if they fight at the king's command. We join the debate

---

1. William Shakespeare, *Henry V*, 4.0.

---

after Williams takes exception to something the king says and rebukes him for it (not knowing he's the king).

> KING HENRY: Your reproof is something too round. I should be angry with you, if the time were convenient.
> WILLIAMS: Let it be a quarrel between us, if you live.
> KING HENRY: I embrace it.
> WILLIAMS: How shall I know thee again?
> KING HENRY: Give me any gage of thine, and I will wear it in my bonnet. Then if ever thou darest acknowledge it, I will make it my quarrel.
> WILLIAMS: Here's my glove. Give me another of thine.
> KING HENRY: There.
> [*They exchange gloves.*]
> WILLIAMS: This will I also wear in my cap. If ever thou come to me and say, after tomorrow, "This is my glove," by this hand I will take thee a box on the ear.
> KING HENRY: If ever I live to see it, I will challenge it.
> WILLIAMS: Thou darest as well be hanged.
> KING HENRY: Well, I will do it, though I take thee in the King's company.[2]

Can you help smiling at Shakespeare's irony? This quarrel could never have happened if the king had appeared to Williams in regal robes, crowned, and with his retinue. Williams would never have threatened to box the ears of his lord and sovereign!

Another King, Another Cloak

If the rulers of this age had known that the man Jesus was the King of all, "they would not have crucified the Lord of glory"

2. Shakespeare, 4.1.

(1 Cor. 2:8). None of the sufferings of Christ that we surveyed in the previous chapter would have been possible if he hadn't hidden his royal glory under the cloak of the Man of Sorrows. But after he completed his suffering on the cross, the cloak was stripped away—he rose from the dead and ascended to heaven to take his rightful place at the right hand of the Majesty on high. Theologians call this his *exaltation*. It was the revelation or *uncloaking* of his glory.

Everything the Old Testament prophets predicted about Christ pointed either to his suffering or to his exaltation.

> Concerning this salvation, the prophets who prophesied about the grace that was to be yours searched and inquired carefully, inquiring what person or time the Spirit of Christ in them was indicating when he predicted the *sufferings* of Christ and the subsequent *glories*. (1 Peter 1:10–11).

So when Christ opened the Scriptures to two disciples on the road to Emmaus, he began by saying, "Was it not necessary that the Christ should *suffer* these things and enter into his *glory*?" (Luke 24:26). Following his Teacher's lead, Paul also sings this chorus.

> Have this mind among yourselves, which is yours in Christ Jesus, who, though he was in the form of God, did not count equality with God a thing to be grasped, but emptied himself, by taking the form of a servant, being born in the likeness of men. And being found in human form, he humbled himself by becoming obedient to the point of death, even death on a cross. Therefore God has highly exalted him and bestowed on him the name that is above every name, so that at the name of Jesus every knee should bow, in heaven and on earth and under the earth, and every tongue confess that Jesus Christ is Lord, to the glory of God the Father. (Phil. 2:5–11)

If we want to know Christ as he is revealed in the Scriptures, we must understand his sufferings—but we must also see that he is now exalted in glory.

Our Own Suffering and Glory

As we reflect on both Christ's suffering and his exaltation, not only will we know him better but we'll "[pluck] comfort from his looks." And we'll need that comfort, because the pattern of *first suffering, then glory* isn't only for Christ but also for us: "The saying is trustworthy, for: If we have died with him, we will also live with him; if we endure, we will also reign with him" (2 Tim. 2:11–12).

It took great courage for Christ to endure his sufferings. He faced them because he knew that before him lay joy beyond measure (Heb. 12:2). If we too are to meet our suffering and not give up, we must look at our Lord, admire his courage, and revel in his exaltation; seeing him in his glory will ennoble our faith. We'll be carried through our own hardships by the certainty that we too will share his glory and joy, as he has promised.

> Let us fix our eyes on Jesus, the author and perfecter of our faith, who for the joy set before him endured the cross, scorning its shame, and sat down at the right hand of the throne of God. Consider him who endured such opposition from sinful men, so that you will not grow weary and lose heart. (Heb. 12:2–3 NIV)

The Lamb of God won our salvation by his suffering and his exaltation. Without these, there would be no church. If he hadn't suffered, our sins wouldn't have been paid for. If he hadn't been exalted, we wouldn't have known whether God had accepted his sacrifice or whether he had defeated death or whether we would be exalted with him.

But he was exalted indeed.

Seeing the Son of Man at the Right Hand of God

Christ prayed in John 17:24 for us to be with him and see his glory. The particular glory he wanted us to see was his exaltation at the right hand of the Father. It wasn't the only glory he wanted us to see, but his exaltation is the way all of his glories become magnified in our eyes.

All the glory of Christ that we've looked at so far was under a cloak while he was in the world. But in his exaltation the cloak is ripped away so that we can see the wonder of who he is and all he did. And when he appears and we see him as he is, what we'll see is this exalted glory (1 John 3:2): the glory that the Father gave him before the foundation of the world (John 17:5, 24) and poured out on him when he ascended to heaven to sit at the right hand of God (Luke 22:69; Acts 2:33; Heb. 1:3).

But don't think that the glory of his exaltation is the glory of his *becoming* God. He had always been God and couldn't *not* be God. The glory of his deity may have been hidden under the cloak of his humanity while he was in the world, but when he rose on the third day he was "declared with power to be the Son of God by his resurrection from the dead" (Rom. 1:4 NIV). This *declaration* of his glory is called his exaltation.

A total eclipse doesn't reduce, by a single photon, the natural beauty and light of the sun. During the eclipse, to us on earth the sun looks dark and dead, but when it emerges from behind the moon, it again shines with its original glory. In the same way, the divine nature of Christ was "eclipsed" when he took the "form of a servant" (Phil. 2:7) and became a poor and despised man in this world. But the eclipse is over. His glory now shines in all its infinite luster. And when those who knew him here as a "man of sorrows" saw him in all the boundless glory of the divine nature, their souls burst with joy and admiration. This is one reason he prayed for them to be with him and to see his glory: he knew what unqualified satisfaction it would be to them forever.

The Glory of Christ's Exaltation

Many masters have tried to paint the Lamb on the throne at the right hand of the Father. But how can we imagine the splendor of this scene? Paint all the gold crowns you like; make the light streaming from Christ as bright as a thousand suns; surround him with crowds of men and angels stretching into the infinite distance. As stunning as such a picture might be under the brush of Rembrandt or Van Eyck, it would be a foggy London morning compared to what we'll see on the day of Christ's glory.

In the same way, my words can barely hint at the true glory of the exalted Lamb. How can I describe his glory? He is exalted over the whole creation in power, dignity, authority, and rule. He rules the universe—not just as God but as man. Speaking of Christ, Paul says, "For by him all things were created, in heaven and on earth, visible and invisible, whether thrones or dominions or rulers or authorities—all things were created through him and for him" (Col. 1:16).

He is exalted by the love and approval of the Father. The Father delights in his Son and is so pleased with his work as Mediator that he has given him the seat of honor at his right hand. There's only one seat at the right hand of the Majesty on high, and that seat was reserved for no other creature. It is an unparalleled honor.

He is the radiance of the glory of God and the exact imprint of his nature, and he upholds the universe by the word of his power. After making purification for sins, he sat down at the right hand of the Majesty on high, having become as much superior to angels as the name he has inherited is more excellent than theirs. (Heb. 1:3–4)

His exaltation fully and finally uncovers and broadcasts the divine wisdom, love, and grace he poured into his work to redeem his bride, the church. Again, no angels or men share one bit of his glory. Because we can see it here only by faith, we see it vaguely, as in an old mirror; but in heaven it is radiant in its brightness, to the unfading joy of all who see him.

> Then I looked, and I heard around the throne and the living creatures and the elders the voice of many angels, numbering myriads of myriads and thousands of thousands, saying with a loud voice,
>
> > "Worthy is the Lamb who was slain,
> > to receive power and wealth and wisdom and might
> > and honor and glory and blessing!" (Rev. 5:11–12)

Seeing the Exalted Christ

Since we're on earth, how can we see glory of the exalted Christ as he is on his throne in heaven? Once again, the only way is by clinging in faith to God's revelation of Christ's glory in his Word. To constantly meditate on his wisdom and love and sufferings and exaltation is an exercise that strengthens our faith; such reflection feeds our faith and makes it flourish.

But what do we tend to fix our minds on? Where do our minds run when they're free from the necessary responsibilities of life? I confess that my mind is eager to sprint from one end of the earth to the other but slow to lift its gaze to heaven. In fact, most of my thoughts hover around my own ego like the Tarleton twins around Scarlett O'Hara.

But what if I put aside all those thoughts about me, me, me and fix my mind on Christ as he is seated at the right hand of the Majesty on high? What if I memorize passages from Colossians and Hebrews and Romans and reflect on what it means for all the creatures of heaven and earth to bow before this man who hung on a cross for me? Or if I consider that this exalted one, who is loved and approved by the Father, is the very one who said that he wants me to be with him where he is (John 14:3; 17:24)? What keeps me from getting carried away with my Savior?

If we believe in Christ, don't we prefer him above ourselves? Don't we rest in his works of righteousness, rather than in our own, and in the suffering he endured in our place? Then faith, if it is true to Christ and not just a figment of our imaginations, should easily trade thoughts of ourselves for thoughts of the Lamb.

Do you need something to stoke your interest in Christ? Ask yourself some questions: Who is exalted over all? Who is surrounded by glory, majesty, and power? Who is enthroned at the right hand of the Majesty on high and resting his feet on all his enemies? Isn't it he who in this world was poor, despised, persecuted, and slain—all for our sake? Isn't it the same Jesus who loved us, and gave himself for us, and washed us in his own blood? Peter told the Jews that "God exalted" the same Jesus whom they slew and hanged on a tree "at his right hand as Leader and Savior, to give repentance to Israel and forgiveness of sins" (Acts 5:30–31). If we value his love, if we value what he did and suffered for his church, we can't help but rejoice in his glory.

Blessed Jesus! We can add nothing to your glory. But to our great joy you are what you are—you are gloriously exalted at the right hand of God. We long to behold your glory more fully and clearly, as you prayed and promised. Amen.

For Reflection and Discussion

1. Christ is the Bridegroom of the church, his beautiful bride. With this in mind, answer the question that is posed in Song of Songs 5:9: "What is your beloved more than another beloved, O most beautiful among women?"

2. What do you think it means that Christ was "exalted at the right hand of God" (Acts 2:33)? Why did God exalt him? What does it mean that he is at God's right hand?

3. Do you think it's true that meditating on Christ in his suffering and exaltation can comfort you and give you hope amid your own suffering? If so, how?

4. Pick a passage of Scripture that describes the exalted Christ (such as Ps. 110; Col. 1:15–29; Heb. 1; or Rev. 4 or 5). Meditate on it every day this week; memorize it if you can. At the end of the week, write a brief prayer of praise to Christ, focusing on details of his exaltation and on your response to it.

8

the center of the old testament

Ex umbris et imaginibus in veritatem.
(From shadows and types to reality.)
—JOHN HENRY NEWMAN

A Master Teacher

As I described in the first chapter, my first year of seminary was intoxicating. Especially those first few weeks, I must have looked like a zombie as I walked back to our apartment for lunch every day. The ideas in my head were spinning out of control. At home, I would lean back in our old gray recliner and stare into infinity. And infinity kept my mind reeling till food brought me back to earth.

My last class before lunch was an introduction to the historical books of the Old Testament. Every day I saw something new. I saw the significance and relevance of passages and stories that I had previously considered to be, at best, some inspiring tales—and, at worst, mystifying. And I was learning how to mine treasures from them as well as gaining new tools and the skills to use them.

Some people might think that this class was great because we were, after all, studying the Bible. But I had lots of other Bible classes that year—and while, yes, they were great, none of them affected me quite the way this one did. The difference in this class was its teacher, Richard Pratt. He knew what to teach and what to leave to the textbooks, and he taught in a way that made us want to learn. He didn't just show us new things; he showed us how to see old things in a new way that made better sense. And he didn't just show us things in a new way but gave us glasses so that we could see things in a new way long after we left his classroom. Richard was a master teacher, and, whether you're studying the Scriptures or finish carpentry or the metaphysical poets, a master teacher makes all the difference.

Didn't Our Hearts Burn?

What would you give to have been with Cleopas and the other disciple as they walked along "looking sad" on the road to Emmaus (Luke 24:13–32)? They were confused and discouraged because they had known Jesus as "a prophet mighty in deed and word before God and all the people" (v. 19) and "had hoped that he was the one to redeem Israel" (v. 21), and yet the "chief priests and rulers delivered him up to be condemned to death, and crucified him" (v. 20). As these two downcast disciples tried to figure all this out, they were met by someone they didn't recognize (v. 16). As he joined their conversation, they were amazed that he seemed to know none of the latest news about Jesus of Nazareth and what had happened during the past few days (v. 18). But then the stranger turned the conversation and their entire world upside down.

> And he said to them, "O foolish ones, and slow of heart to believe all that the prophets have spoken! Was it not neces- sary that the Christ should suffer these things and enter into

114

his glory?" And beginning with Moses and all the Prophets, he interpreted to them in all the Scriptures the things concerning himself. (vv. 25–27)

Later, this extraordinary stranger sat down to dinner with them. He broke the bread, and suddenly they recognized him: their new teacher was in fact their old Teacher. It was Jesus, the Master, raised from the dead. In a heartbeat, he disappeared (vv. 28–31). I imagine they were breathless, and that their minds were spinning farther out of control than mine was in my gray recliner, as they turned to each other and said, "Did not our hearts burn within us while he talked to us on the road, while he opened to us the Scriptures?" (v. 32).

If only I could have been there! Jesus was the Master of master teachers, and he unfolded to his disciples the world-changing mystery of how he, the Christ, was the subject of the entire Old Testament. He began with Moses (the first five books of the Bible) and traced what was said about him all the way through the Prophets—he showed them how the Old Testament, from beginning to end, spoke of the Christ.

Christ is the line of life and light that runs through the whole Old Testament. Only by seeing him in its pages can we fully grasp its meaning and significance. If we neglect to look for him there, we'll be as blind while reading it as the unbelieving Jews, who read it with a veil over their minds. Only faith that discovers the glory of Christ can remove that veil of darkness (2 Cor. 3:14–16). So let's look at some of the ways that the glory of Christ was represented to believers in the Old Testament.

Christ the Glorious Tabernacle

Can you name the first person in the Bible who is said to be full of the Holy Spirit? He is introduced in Exodus 31: Bezalel, son of Uri.

The LORD said to Moses, "See, I have called by name Bezalel the son of Uri, son of Hur, of the tribe of Judah, and I have filled him with the Spirit of God, with ability and intelligence, with knowledge and all craftsmanship, to devise artistic designs, to work in gold, silver, and bronze, in cutting stones for setting, and in carving wood, to work in every craft. And behold, I have appointed with him Oholiab, the son of Ahisamach, of the tribe of Dan. And I have given to all able men ability, that they may make all that I have commanded you: the tent of meeting, and the ark of the testimony, and the mercy seat that is on it, and all the furnishings of the tent, the table and its utensils, and the pure lampstand with all its utensils, and the altar of incense, and the altar of burnt offering with all its utensils, and the basin and its stand, and the finely worked garments, the holy garments for Aaron the priest and the garments of his sons, for their service as priests, and the anointing oil and the fragrant incense for the Holy Place. According to all that I have commanded you, they shall do." (Ex. 31:1–11)

The ceremonies of worship in the Old Testament were complex and mysterious. They were designed by God's wisdom and were important enough for him to fill an artist with his Spirit to make the objects that would be used to perform the ceremonies. The forms of worship commanded by God became the center of Israel's life, because it was through them that God showed his people the glory of the Christ who was to come.

What were the tabernacle and temple? What were the Holy Place and its utensils? What were the ark, the cherubim, the mercy seat? What was the high priest in all his vestments and duties? What were the sacrifices and the annual sprinkling of blood in the Most Holy Place? What was the whole system of their worship ceremonies? They were holy representations of Christ in his glory as God and man and his glory as our Mediator and Redeemer.

They were a shadow—and the body that cast the shadow was Christ (see Heb. 8–9).

Before we try to see Christ's glory as it was conveyed by Old Testament ceremonies and instruments of worship, we need some encouragement that will help us to get over any distrust of symbolism:

> We in the West aren't very much at ease with symbolism ourselves. We live in an industrialized society dominated by scientific and technological forms of knowledge. Such knowledge minimizes the play of metaphors and the personal depth dimensions of human living. For many people, "real" truth means technological truth, that is, truth swept free of metaphor and symbolism. We meet symbolism mostly in advertising, and such use of symbolism rouses our suspicions and often ends by producing indifference.
>
> I am convinced that God does not share our general cultural aversion to metaphors and symbols. He wrote the Old Testament, which contains a good deal of poetry and many uses of metaphor. . . . We must adapt to the fact that symbols and metaphors can speak truly and powerfully without speaking with pedantic scientific precision. A symbol may suggest a deep truth or even a cluster of related truths without blurting everything out in plain talk and making everything crystal clear. An element of mystery may remain, because a symbol can suggest a whole host of connections.[1]

In other words, this exercise of reflecting on the glory of the Lamb of God as he's pictured in Israel's worship might leave us not only confused and tentative but even a bit skeptical. But

---

1. Vern S. Poythress, *The Shadow of Christ in the Law of Moses* (Brentwood, TN: Wolgemuth & Hyatt, 1991; Phillipsburg, NJ: P&R Publishing, 1995), 38.

the book of Hebrews makes clear that any such problem is ours. Commentators who are tuned in to biblical symbolism can help us along the path of seeing Christ in the tabernacle.

For example, consider what two pieces of the tabernacle's furniture reveal about Christ.

The Lampstand

The perpetual light of the lampstand in the Holy Place pointed to the true Light that was coming into the world (Ex. 27:20–21; Lev. 24:1–4). The lamp was continually filled with oil (as Christ was continually filled with the Spirit) so that it illuminated the tabernacle day and night. It reminded worshippers of God, their Creator and Redeemer. As Creator, he made the light shine out of the darkness (Gen. 1:1–3), and as Redeemer, he was the pillar of fire by night that led them out of Egypt and through the wilderness to the promised land (Ex. 13:21). This imagery points to Christ, who is our Creator and Redeemer (Col. 1:15–20), the light that shines in our dark souls to recreate us (2 Cor. 4:6), and the true light that shines through spiritual darkness to make the blind see (John 1:5, 9; 8:12; 9:3–6).

We could go farther with the lampstand and its imagery: consider its shape—a tree with branches and almond flowers— and see in it Christ, who is the Tree of Life, and the fruitfulness of his light that gives new life to the world. But these few suggestions are only meant to prime the pump of your own reflection on Christ.

The Bread of the Presence

The bread of the presence pointed to the true Bread that was coming down from heaven (Ex. 25:23–30). This bread symbolized the presence of God, the gracious host of a meal and his worshippers as his honored guests whom he would feed and protect. It reminded them of the manna he had given them day after day in the wilderness and of its sweet taste—a symbol of God's goodness and of his daily provision. Jesus made it plain that he was the substance that cast the shadow, the true Bread of the Presence.

> Jesus then said to them, "Truly, truly, I say to you, it was not Moses who gave you the bread from heaven, but my Father gives you the true bread from heaven. For the bread of God is he who comes down from heaven and gives life to the world. . . .
>
> I am the bread of life; whoever comes to me shall not hunger, and whoever believes in me shall never thirst." (John 6:32–33, 35)

Take these few suggestive paragraphs as your starting point, and look for Christ within the worship of the Old Testament. Let the New Testament guide you into a deeper understanding of the richness of the imagery.[2] The sum of that imagery is that "Moses was faithful in all God's house as a servant, to testify to the things that were to be spoken later" (Heb. 3:5). That is, all that Moses did, when he built the tabernacle and instituted its services, was a preview of the things of Christ that were later revealed. These dark but glorious views of Christ were the life of the Old Testament church.

Christ the Glorious Lover

Marriage has always represented the spiritual intimacy that God shares with his people through love, kindness, joy, and

---

2. See, for example, John 1:29, 36; 6:32–35; 1 Corinthians 5:7; Colossians 2:17; Hebrews 4:14–16; 5:1–10; 8:2; 9:7–15, 18–28; 10:19–22; 13:10–13; 1 Peter 1:18–19. Ask your pastor to recommend a commentary on Hebrews that can prompt and guide your reflection.

faithfulness. "For as a young man marries a young woman, so shall your sons marry you, and as the bridegroom rejoices over the bride, so shall your God rejoice over you" (Isa. 62:5).[3]

The Song of Songs is a glorious display of the love between a bride and groom, and the church has always seen in it an analogy of the tenderness God shows to his people and of his people's exuberant love for their God. In the New Testament, Christ reveals that he is that Groom (John 3:29; Rev. 21:9), and Paul explains that marriage is a mystical picture of Christ and his bride.

> "Therefore a man shall leave his father and mother and hold fast to his wife, and the two shall become one flesh." This mystery is profound, and *I am saying that it refers to Christ and the church.* (Eph. 5:31–32)

Many who have drawn close to Christ see their closeness to him described in the intimacy depicted in the Song of Songs. Again, our discomfort and lack of skill with metaphor, imagery, and typology may make us overcautious about reading ourselves and Christ into this love song. But centuries of faithful saints who have gone before us felt no such inhibitions. Even our sober-minded Puritan fathers and mothers, who are such a faithful corrective to so many of the church's excesses in our day, let fly with a lover's abandon as they relish the glory of Christ our Bridegroom as he is revealed in the Song of Songs.

Joyous interpretation of the Song of Songs didn't die with the Puritans. Consider "Jesus Christ the Apple Tree," a traditional American Christmas song that meditates on the Bridegroom in Song of Songs 2:3. This song shows us a way we can explore and savor the implications of a single image of Christ and can unfold from it layer after layer of his glory.

---

3. See also, for example, Isaiah 49:8; 61:10; Jeremiah 2:2; Ezekiel 16:8–14.

Jesus Christ the Apple Tree

The tree of life my soul hath seen,
Laden with fruit, and always green:
The trees of nature fruitless be
Compared with Christ the apple tree.

His beauty doth all things excel:
By faith I know, but ne'er can tell
The glory which I now can see
In Jesus Christ the apple tree.

For happiness I long have sought,
And pleasure dearly I have bought:
I missed of all; but now I see
'Tis found in Christ the apple tree.

I'm weary with my former toil,
Here I will sit and rest awhile:
Under the shadow I will be,
Of Jesus Christ the apple tree.

This fruit doth make my soul to thrive,
It keeps my dying faith alive;
Which makes my soul in haste to be
With Jesus Christ the apple tree.[4]

4. From *Divine Hymns or Spiritual Songs*, comp. Joshua Smith (New Hampshire, 1784). This song and its source in Song of Songs 2:3 inspired the drawing that appears in the frontispiece.

Drawing on the shadows and images of the glory of the Lamb in the tabernacle and temple, and the Song of Songs' representation of his beauty and grace and love, we have an idea of the depth of Christ's glory that the saints of the Old Testament could see. We have no need to pity them when we see these holy choruses of delight and admiration, these raptures of joy, this ardent affection. God provided them ways to commune with him—ways for those who believed to discover the glory of Christ. Time spent reflecting on them is a pleasure that excels all that the world has to offer.

Christ the Glorious Angel of the Lord

Christ appeared several times to leaders of the church in the Old Testament. This was a prelude to his incarnation, but he appeared in the shape of a man to show what he would be. He didn't create a human nature and unite it to himself as a kind of "temporary incarnation"; by his divine power, he took the form of a man and immediately dissolved it when he finished with it. In this way he appeared to Abraham, to Jacob, to Moses, to Joshua, and to others.[5]

And because Christ was the divine person who lived in and with the church from the beginning to the end of the Old Testament, he often demonstrated human affections to hint that a time would come when he would take on our nature. Indeed, we might almost say that after the fall nothing is said about God in the Old Testament except what relates to the future incarnation of Christ. It makes sense that God is represented so often as a man grieving, repenting, and being angry or pleased, since he intended to take on a human nature that was capable of such passions and affections.

5. See Charles Hodge, *Systematic Theology* (1871; repr., Grand Rapids: Eerdmans, 1982), 1:484–95.

Christ the Glorious Vision

The prophets saw the glory of Christ in visions. John says that Isaiah "saw [Jesus's] glory and spoke of him" (John 12:41), referring to Isaiah's spectacular vision of Christ's glory filling and spilling out of the temple (Isa. 6:1–5). He saw the fullness of God overflowing from the body of the man Christ (cf. Col. 2:9), the temple that he would destroy and rebuild in three days (John 2:19–21). When he saw this, Isaiah was overcome by dread. He was revived only by the ministry of that glorious One, when his sin was burned from him with a coal from the altar—all of which was symbolic of the sacrifice and atonement of the Lamb to come (Isa. 6:6–7). This was (and is) food for the souls of believers.

Christ the Glorious Promise

Countless promises throughout the Old Testament expound the coming incarnation of Christ and his glory.

> For to us a child is born,
>   to us a son is given;
> and the government shall be upon his shoulder,
>   and his name shall be called
> Wonderful Counselor, Mighty God,
>   Everlasting Father, Prince of Peace.
> Of the increase of his government and of peace
>   there will be no end,
> on the throne of David and over his kingdom,
>   to establish it and to uphold it
> with justice and with righteousness
>   from this time forth and forevermore.
> The zeal of the Lord of hosts will do this. (Isa. 9:6–7)

When these promises were given, they weren't as clear as they are now; but we can now see how they were fulfilled, and we have the apostles and Christ to explain them to us. Christ exactly answered all the promises regarding when and where he would be born, what kind of man he would be, how he would suffer and die and rise from the dead. All these promises are so clear that only unbelief and pride keep anyone from seeing Christ's glory in them.

Christ the Glorious Lily, Lamb, and Lion

The Old Testament brims with metaphors that show the glory of Christ. Our Lord is called a Lily to show his gracious beauty in comparison to others (Song 2:1–2). He is called a Rose for the sweet savor of his love, grace, and obedience (Song 2:1). He is a Lamb who is meek and gentle—fit to be a sacrifice (Gen. 22:8)—and he is a powerful Lion (Isa. 31:4).

Poets use metaphors because they not only tell; they *show and tell*. That is, they make a stronger impression on the mind and heart than abstract descriptions. For example, "The LORD is my Shepherd" engraves in our minds something deep that would be impossible to equal with an essay about God as a provider and protector. Metaphors appeal to more of our senses and compel us to work at understanding them, even to *play* at uncovering their richness. So it makes sense that God, in his wisdom, represents powerful spiritual truth to us through natural images from the world around us. And rolling a metaphor around in your mind can be a delicious way of tasting and relishing the glory of Christ.

Christ the Glorious Center

Christ was the center of the Old Testament. All the promises, prophecies, and predictions about who he would be, when he would come, what he would do—along with the wisdom, grace, and love that God showed to the church through him—are the lifeline that runs through all the Hebrew Scriptures. These were the sorts of things he opened to his disciples out of Moses and all the Prophets (Luke 24). These were the things he appealed to as he confronted his enemies: "You search the Scriptures because you think that in them you have eternal life; and *it is they that bear witness about me*" (John 5:39). If we can't find him in their pages, it's because a veil covers our minds. And we can't read, study, or meditate on the Old Testament to any advantage unless we try to find and behold the glory of Christ in them. Without Christ, the Old Testament is a closed book.

This chapter is but a thimble from the ocean of the glory of the Christ that is seen in the pages of the Old Testament. Remember how Christ showed the disciples that he was the theme that ran from Moses through the Prophets, and take this chapter's brief hints into your own reflections. Let the glory of Christ blaze from the dusty old pages of Leviticus and Chronicles, Numbers and Lamentations, until you join with Moses and David and Isaiah in singing songs of glory to the Lamb.

For Reflection and Discussion

1. Christ is the Bridegroom of the church, his beautiful bride. With this in mind, answer the question that is posed in Song of Songs 5:9: "What is your beloved more than another beloved, O most beautiful among women?"

2. Choose a metaphor from the Old Testament that refers to Christ. Choose one of those mentioned in this chapter or one of the following:

Branch from Jesse (Isa. 11:1)	Fountain (Zech. 13:1)
Everlasting Father (Isa. 9:6)	Servant (Isa. 52:13–15)
Prince of Peace (Isa. 9:6)	Sure Foundation (Isa. 28:16)

Spend time reflecting on that metaphor and on how it unveils the glory of Christ. Then write a brief prayer of praise to Christ that flows from the metaphor.

3. Use the song "Jesus Christ the Apple Tree," from earlier in this chapter, to guide your reflection on Christ. What are some aspects of his glory that it depicts?

4. Choose one of the pieces of furniture that was in the tabernacle, other than the lampstand or the bread of the presence, and write four or five sentences about how it might have represented something of the glory of the Messiah to believers during the days of Moses. (Refer to Exodus 25–30.)

9

by just exchange

My true love hath my heart and I have his,
    By just exchange one for the other giv'n;
I hold his dear, and mine he cannot miss,
    There never was a better bargain driv'n.
—Sir Philip Sidney

An Unjust Exchange

Jean Valjean, the hero of *Les Misérables*, is a former convict running from his miserable past and from the undaunted Inspector Javert. After many years, he is offered an extraordinary chance to escape both his past and Javert forever: Another convicted criminal, Champmathieu, is mistakenly identified as Jean Valjean and put on trial. Three prisoners swear in court that Champmathieu is Jean Valjean, so it's certain he'll be falsely convicted and punished. All Jean Valjean need do to be free is say nothing.

Jean Valjean is tempted to let the man suffer in his place. After all, he reasons, Champmathieu is a criminal and deserves to be punished anyway. Jean Valjean could be free from Javert's dogged pursuit; he could be free to do the good he now plans to do—to care for the forsaken Fantine and her daughter, Cosette; he could continue to help his city prosper. All these good things would be impossible if he walked into the courtroom and cleared Champmathieu and surrendered to the law.

But the thought of another man suffering in his place was too much; Jean Valjean was overwhelmed by the injustice of it. He realized that by letting even this wretch take his punishment, "he was becoming a robber once more, and the most odious of robbers! he was robbing another man of his existence, his livelihood, his peace, and his place in the sunshine. He was becoming an assassin, he was killing, morally killing, a wretched man; he was inflicting on him the frightful living death, the open-air death, which is called the galleys."[1] In spite of all he stood to gain and all the good he could do, Jean Valjean could not let Champmathieu suffer in his place.

The injustice of a person suffering for someone else's crimes burns our consciences. Yet if you grew up in the church, the first thing you learned is that "*Christ died for our sins*" (1 Cor. 15:3). And I hope that at some point in your life, the phrase "Christ died for *me*" became precious to you. If that is your story, maybe the phrase "Christ died for our sins" has never struck you as odd.

But think about it. *We* did something terribly wrong, and *someone else* suffered for it. Does that bother you? Imagine you're a ten-year-old in a family that owns only one bike, and you and your sister are expected to share it by each taking a turn every half hour. Your sister, on one of those days when a person just feels mean, has been on the bike for an hour straight. She wheels slowly by, her tongue stuck out, silently baiting you *Whatcha gonna do about it?*, and you throw up your hands in dismay. Just

---

1. Victor Hugo, *Les Misérables*, trans. Lascelles Wraxall (repr., New York: The Heritage Press, 1938) 1:223.

as Dad comes outside, your sister yells, "Loser!" Dad immediately passes sentence: no biking for a month—for *you*.

Feel the injustice?

When put that way, it sounds wrong. Yet our eternal hopes hang on the fact that someone else paid for the evil we did. Peter tells us that "[Christ] himself bore our sins in his body on the tree" (1 Peter 2:24) and that "Christ also suffered once for sins, the righteous for the unrighteous, that he might bring us to God" (1 Peter 3:18). Our sense of justice balks at the thought of a good man dying for an evil man. And the Bible clearly lays the "blame" for this at God's feet: "*The Lord* has laid on him the iniquity of us all" (Isa. 53:6). If this is an injustice, what does that say about God's character? How can he be the Judge of the world if he is unjust in handing out punishment?

The Scriptures answer all such objections and vindicate God's righteousness. It wasn't just "okay" for Christ to suffer for the sins of his people; it was right and good and just. The Scriptures teach that there's a union between Christ and his people—a union so intimate that God considers everything that Christ did and suffered as if we did and suffered it. Therefore, God is right to let us off the hook for our sins, as if we had already paid the penalty for them in full, and to shower us with rewards as if we had perfectly obeyed his law. Understanding this just exchange is a way for us to strengthen our faith and see the glory of Christ.

To understand the problem and how God solved it, we need some background. All of God's chosen people, as members of humanity, came under God's curse when Adam sinned (Rom. 5:12–21). This curse meant certain death, including the eternal death of hell. It was impossible for God to simply sweep our sins under the rug. He would have had to deny his own righteousness, holiness, and truth. As Moses put it, "He does not leave the guilty unpunished" (Ex. 34:7 NIV). So in order for God to save his people, yet at the same time remain just and holy, he had to find someone else who could bear the weight of the curse for them.

This idea of a substitute taking the punishment for God's people is the cornerstone of the gospel, and it's taught from Genesis through Revelation. God hinted at it in his first gospel promise, when he said that the Messiah would suffer (the serpent would "bruise his heel," Gen. 3:15); he later spelled it out through the sacrifices and ceremonies of worship he gave to the people through Moses. This is the most important thing God's people were to learn from these sacrifices: that their guilt would have to be transferred to another for them to escape the punishment they deserved.[2]

By Just Exchange

God can do only what is right (Gen. 18:25). We can know what's right by watching what he does. This God, who does only right, has often punished some people for the sins of others. Therefore, it is just to do this, at least in some cases. In fact, God makes it plain in the Ten Commandments that he does this: "I the LORD your God am a jealous God, visiting the iniquity of the fathers on the children to the third and the fourth generation of those who hate me" (Ex. 20:5). Jeremiah affirms that this happens: "Our fathers sinned, and are no more; and we bear their iniquities" (Lam. 5:7).

Many examples show that these cases of substitutionary punishment aren't exceptions. When God sent Judah into captivity in Babylon, he punished them for the sins of their ancestors—particularly the sins that were committed in the days of Manasseh (2 Kings 23:26–27). God cursed Canaan for the

---

2. This is why the priest was to lay his hand on the head of the sacrifice, symbolizing the transfer of the guilt of the people to the animal (see Lev. 3–4).

sin of his father, Ham (Gen. 9:25). Saul's seven sons were put to death for their father's bloody cruelty (2 Sam. 21:5–6, 9, 14). God sent an angel to destroy seventy thousand people for the king's sin, even though David said, "I am the one who has sinned and done wrong. These are but sheep. What have they done? Let your hand fall upon me and my family" (2 Sam. 24:15–17). In spite of the legendary wickedness of Ahab, God said of him, "Have you seen how Ahab has humbled himself before me? Because he has humbled himself before me, I will not bring the disaster in his days; but in his son's days I will bring the disaster upon his house" (1 Kings 21:29). It was the same for the children and infants who were destroyed in the flood or in the fires of Sodom and Gomorrah. And Jesus said that when God cut off the nation of Israel, he was punishing that final generation for all the bloody persecutions of the prophets from the beginning of the world.

> Therefore this generation will be held responsible for the blood of all the prophets that has been shed since the beginning of the world, from the blood of Abel to the blood of Zechariah, who was killed between the altar and the sanctuary. Yes, I tell you, this generation will be held responsible for it all. (Luke 11:50–51 NIV)

Each of these demonstrates God's terrifying justice. They clearly teach that our righteous, true, and holy God will sometimes punish some people for the sins of others. Therefore, at least in some cases, this can't be wrong.

When Is This Exchange Just?

So it isn't always wrong to punish someone for the sins of others; yet neither is it always right. There has to be a peculiar connection or union between those who sin and those who are punished. This union must include an *intimate relationship* and a *close mutual interest.*

The intimate relationship must be as close as the relationship between parents and children, as it was in most of the examples we've seen in the Scriptures, or between a king and his subjects, as in the case of David. In these cases, the sinners and the sufferers are treated as one body, so that the backside answers for what the hand steals. And those who sin must have a close mutual interest with those who are punished for their sins—so close an interest that they feel the punishment themselves, the way a father would be tormented to see his son suffer.

Imagine what you would feel if God said to you, as he said to his grumbling people in the wilderness, "And your children shall be shepherds in the wilderness forty years and shall suffer for your faithlessness, until the last of your dead bodies lies in the wilderness" (Num. 14:33). Wouldn't you grieve at the thought of what your sins had brought on your children? That would be the sting of your own punishment.

We can distinguish three ways in which people can be joined in an intimate relationship: by a natural union, by a spiritual or mystical union, or by an agreed union (such as a covenant). Christ is singularly united to us through all three. His union with the church is more intimate, and holds more mutual interest, than any other relationship. Because of this, it was just and right for God to slay the Lamb for our sins and to count his suffering and death as our own.

Our Natural Union with Christ

God made all people "from one man" (Acts 17:26), and thus there is an alliance among us all. All people are our brothers or sisters or neighbors and are due our kindness (Luke 10:36). By his incarnation, Christ shared this natural union with us in order to save his church:

Since therefore the children share in flesh and blood, he himself likewise partook of the same things, that through death he might destroy the one who has the power of death, that is, the devil, and deliver all those who through fear of death were subject to lifelong slavery. (Heb. 2:14–15)

So "both the one who makes men holy and those who are made holy are of the same family" (Heb. 2:11 NIV). And although his union with us in our humanity is "natural," two things distinguish the union we have with him from the natural union we have with all people.

First, this natural union between Christ and the church came about not by nature but by a voluntary act of his will. Our union with others is necessary. We are all brothers and sisters because we are human beings. It's a fact of life and has nothing to do with choice. With the Lord Christ, it was different (Heb. 2:11, 14–15). So that he might rescue us from death, he freely and humbly chose to take on our flesh and blood. He is united to the church through his own free choice. It is thus right for him to suffer for those whose nature he shares.

Second, Christ took on our flesh in order to obey and suffer in the place of the church. Hebrews 2:14–15 says he took our flesh "*that* through death he might destroy the one who has the power of death . . . and deliver all those who through fear of death were subject to lifelong slavery."This was the only reason for his natural union with the church; and this makes his union with us incomparably closer than any other union.

Our Spiritual Union with Christ

Some things are united physically, such as the head of a body and its hands or the trunk of a tree and its branches. But people may be united in a *moral* or *spiritual* sense, as in the case of a husband and a wife. The Scriptures teach that such a union between Christ and his church is the foundation of his suffering in our place. In Ephesians 5, Paul calls the church Christ's bride and says that he "gave himself up for her" (v. 25). Since he was the head and husband of the church, the only way he could sanctify and save her was by his blood and suffering—and it was righteous that what he did and suffered should be considered our own.

Our Contractual or Covenantal Union with Christ

People can be joined by legal instruments, such as a power of attorney or a contract with an agent, which allow them to designate someone else to act on their behalf. Christ was united to us through a similar bond that the Father made with him.

> And it was not without an oath. For those who formerly became priests were made such without an oath, but this one was made a priest with an oath by the one who said to him:
>
> > "The LORD has sworn
> >   and will not change his mind,
> > 'You are a priest forever.'"
>
> This makes Jesus the guarantor of a better covenant. (Heb. 7:20–22)

Through this covenantal bond, which was sealed by God's oath, Christ took it on himself to suffer in our place, and on our behalf, so that he would give to God whatever he required from us in order to save and sanctify us. Because of this contract, it was perfectly just for him to be punished for our sins.

This is the holy mystery of how the guilt and punishment of the sins of the church were transferred to One who was in every way innocent and righteous. This just exchange is the life, soul, and center of the gospel. By this exchange Christ becomes immeasurably glorious and precious to us who believe. No heart can conceive, no tongue can express, the glory of Christ in his suffering for our sake.

There Never Was a Better Bargain Driv'n

We've already looked at the infinite humility and love the Lamb showed by obeying and suffering for us, so now let's consider the greatness of this union that we see in some of its fruit.

This Union Exalts the Righteousness of God in Forgiving Sins

The justice of God's rule and government constitute some of our highest thoughts. It is God's right to punish sin as it deserves, and punishing sin was one of the first things he did to govern his creation. First he punished Satan and the angels who joined his rebellion, then he expelled Adam and Eve from paradise in Eden.

Because of the fall, all God's elect are sinners; we all sinned in Adam, who represented us, and we ourselves continue to sin. What should the God of justice do to us? Should he wink at our crimes and rebellion and leave us all unpunished? If so, how would that square with his justice, which didn't spare Adam in the beginning or even one angel who sinned? The righteousness of God on the one hand, and the forgiveness of sin on the other, seem so contradictory that many stumble over the paradox (see Rom. 10:3–4). How can we reconcile the truth that God "does not leave the guilty unpunished" (Ex. 34:7 NIV) with the statement that God "justifies the ungodly" (Rom. 4:5)?

But when Christ unites himself to the church and takes on her punishment, we see a glorious harmony between God's righteousness and his forgiveness. Because of this union, it was perfectly just that "the LORD . . . laid on him the iniquity of us all" (Isa. 53:6) and that he freely and graciously pardoned us. In the slaying of the Lamb for us we see the highest magnification of the honor of both God's justice and his mercy. Not one of our sins is left unpunished,[3] yet we also revel in his redeeming grace.

> But now the righteousness of God has been manifested apart from the law, although the Law and the Prophets bear witness to it—the righteousness of God through faith in Jesus Christ for all who believe. For there is no distinction: for all have sinned and fall short of the glory of God, and are justified by his grace as a gift, through the redemption that is in Christ Jesus, whom God put forward as a propitiation by his blood, to be received by faith. This was to show God's righteousness, because in his divine forbearance he had passed over former sins. It was to show his righteousness at the present time, so that he might be just and the justifier of the one who has faith in Jesus. (Rom. 3:21–26)

By solving this problem, Christ makes himself glorious in the sight of God, angels, and the church. Through him there is at the same time, in one divine act, a bubbling over of both justice and mercy. The apparent inconsistency between the righteousness of God and the salvation of sinners, which troubles some to the point that they reject Christ and are eternally lost, is removed and taken away.

In his cross, divine holiness and vindictive justice slay the Lamb of God; and out of his triumph gush grace and mercy. This glory ravishes the hearts and satisfies the souls of believers. For what more can we want, what more perfectly calms and steadies our souls, than to see God eternally pleased in the declaration of

---

3. Every sin ever committed is punished—either in Christ as he hangs on the cross for his people or by the sinner in hell forever.

his righteousness and the exercise of his mercy? "In due apprehensions hereof let my soul live—in the faith hereof let me die, and let present admiration of this glory make way for the eternal enjoyment of it in its beauty and fulness."[4]

This Union Is Glorious because in It We See the Perfection of God's Law

When we fell in Adam, we were no longer able to keep the law that God required of us.[5] If his law had been left broken and unfulfilled, no one could ever see God's wisdom, holiness, and righteousness in giving it. What could be less becoming of a perfect God than for him to give a law that could never be fulfilled by its subjects? How would it show his wisdom if he promised eternal rewards for keeping a law that none could ever keep? Although we could never keep it, Christ could—and through his obedience and because of his union with us, the law was fulfilled in us by being fulfilled for us, to the glory of God.

> For God has done what the law, weakened by the flesh, could not do. By sending his own Son in the likeness of sinful flesh and for sin, he condemned sin in the flesh, in order that the righteous requirement of the law might be fulfilled in us, who walk not according to the flesh but according to the Spirit. (Rom. 8:3–4)

When our souls are beaten down with fear and our consciences troubled by temptation and sin, our faith can cling to

---

4. John Owen, *Meditations and Discourses on the Glory of Christ*, reprinted in *The Works of John Owen*, ed. William H. Goold, vol. 1 (Edinburgh: Johnstone & Hunter, 1850; repr., Banner of Truth Trust, 1991), 359.

5. This is the doctrine of *original sin*, the corruption of our nature. For a summary, see Louis Berkhof, *Systematic Theology* (Grand Rapids: Eerdmans, 1941), 244–54.

Christ's obedience. He satisfied every demand of God. Because he is joined to us in this intimate union and has obeyed for us, we have nothing to fear from the most terrifying threats of the law. Through our union with him we have peace that passes understanding.

> By just exchange one for the other giv'n . . .
> There never was a better bargain driv'n.

For Reflection and Discussion

1. Christ is the Bridegroom of the church, his beautiful bride. With this in mind, answer the question that is posed in Song of Songs 5:9: "What is your beloved more than another beloved, O most beautiful among women?"

2. How would you answer an unbeliever (or a troubled believer) who objected to the gospel on the grounds that it was unjust for someone to pay for someone else's crime?

3. What is it that makes Christ's natural union with us closer than the union we share with any other human being?

4. What is it that makes Christ's spiritual union with us closer than the union we share with any other human being?

5. What is it that makes Christ's contractual union with us closer than the union we share with any other human being?

6. What does the oath in Hebrews 7:20–22 mean for your faith?

7. How does Christ solve the apparent conflict between God's mercy and his justice?

Charitas Nimia, or the Dear Bargain

Lord, what is man? why should he cost thee
So dear? what had his ruin lost thee?
Lord, what is man, that thou hast over-bought
      So much a thing of naught?

    Love is too kind, I see, and can
Make but a simple merchantman;
'Twas for such sorry merchandise
Bold painters have put out his eyes.

    Alas, sweet Lord, what were't to thee,
If there were no such worms as we?
Heaven ne'ertheless still heaven would be,
      Should mankind dwell
      In the deep hell,
What have his woes to do with thee?

      Let him go weep
      O'er his own wounds;
      Seraphims will not sleep
Nor spheres let fall their faithful rounds.

    Still would the youthful spirits sing,
And still thy spacious palace ring:
Still would those beauteous ministers of light
      Burn all as bright,

And bow their flaming heads before thee;
Still Thrones and Dominations would adore thee;
Still would those ever-wakeful sons of fire
        Keep warm thy praise
        Both nights and days,
And teach thy loved name to their noble lyre.

        Let froward dust then do its kind,
And give itself for sport to the proud wind.
Why should a piece of peevish care plead shares
In the Eternity of thy old cares?
Why shouldst thou bow thy awful breast to see
What mine own madnesses have done with me?

        Should not the King still keep his throne
Because some desperate fool's undone?
Or will the world's illustrious eyes
Weep for every worm that dies?

        Will the gallant sun
        E'er the less glorious run?
Will he hang down his golden head
Or e'er the sooner seek his western bed,
        Because some foolish fly
        Grows wanton and will die?

        If I were lost in misery,
What was it to thy heaven and thee?
What was it to thy precious blood
If my foul heart called for a flood?

What if my faithless soul and I
    Would needs fall in
    With guilt and sin?
What did the Lamb that he should die?
What did the Lamb that he should need,
When the Wolf sins, himself to bleed?

    If my base lust
Bargained with death and well be-seeming dust,
    Why should the white
    Lamb's bosom write
    The purple name
    Of my sin's shame?

Why should the unstained breast make good
My blushes with his own heart-blood?

O, my Saviour, make me see
How dearly thou hast paid for me,

That lost again my life may prove
As then in death, so now in love.

RICHARD CRASHAW

10

the glory of glories

All the king's horses, and all the king's men,
Couldn't put Humpty together again.
—MOTHER GOOSE

It's hard enough to mend a broken egg. But what if, instead of Humpty Dumpty, it was all the king's men who had a great fall? Could anyone put them back together again? I don't mean sewing arms and legs back on and binding up broken bones. I'm talking about what it would take to restore those who tumbled, with Adam, away from God and his holy angels. I'm talking about making right everything that makes the world groan—from drought and famine to corruption and genocide to perversion and rage.

I'm sure by now you know the only One who's equal to the task. Paul told the Ephesians that God, with all wisdom and understanding, has

> made known to us the mystery of his will according to his good pleasure, which he purposed in Christ, to be put into effect when the times will have reached their fulfillment—*to bring*

all things in heaven and on earth together under one head, even Christ. (Eph. 1:9–10 NIV)

Philosophers, scientists, counselors, and politicians are all trying to patch up everything from global contagion to global conflict. By God's grace, they succeed now and then at restoring peace between two nations, or wiping out smallpox, or helping troubled people to cope with day-to-day life, and we rightly thank God for these gifts. But it is the glory of Christ that he'll one day make *everything* whole again—and make it even better than it was in the beginning.

To better see his glory, let's review the history of the world.

A Tale of Two Families

Try to imagine what it was like before God created the heavens and the earth.

Does your head hurt yet? If not, you're not trying. It's not easy to think away the universe. But if you could, what would be left? *Nothing*. Nothing but God, that is. Before he created anything, God was. Father, Son, and Holy Spirit—one God in three persons—existed from eternity in complete love and harmony and blessedness. And God held within himself all being, power, goodness, wisdom—all the perfections that we now adore in him.

When God made the heavens and the earth, he gave the universe being and goodness by his power and wisdom, and he did this in order to show his glory. This was the first time God gave of himself to anything outside himself, and it was glorious.

The heavens declare the glory of God,
and the sky above proclaims his handiwork. (Ps. 19:1)

For his invisible attributes, namely, his eternal power and divine nature, have been clearly perceived, ever since the creation of the world, in the things that have been made. (Rom. 1:20)

Now, this creation of God's is an elaborate, living system, with interlocking pieces that all depend on one another for their energy and sustenance. These are the ecosystems and symbiotic relationships and food chains and solar systems that we studied in eighth-grade biology and tenth-grade astronomy. But what they didn't teach us in secular science books is that all of these interdependent systems depend on God himself as their eternal fountain of existence, power, and goodness. God is no less glorious in keeping the universe working from moment to moment than he was in creating it all. Take away God's sustaining hand, and the universe disappears without a trace—faster than the lights go out when you flip the switch.

He did good by giving you rains from heaven and fruitful seasons, satisfying your hearts with food and gladness. (Acts 14:17)

The God who made the world and everything in it, being Lord of heaven and earth, does not live in temples made by man, nor is he served by human hands, as though he needed anything, since he himself gives to all mankind life and breath and everything . . . for

"In him we live and move and have our being";

as even some of your own poets have said,

"For we are indeed his offspring." (Acts 17:24–25, 28)

He is the radiance of the glory of God and the exact imprint of his nature, and *he upholds the universe by the word of his power.* (Heb. 1:3)

When God gave existence to his tangible, visible creation, he did it to show us his glory. He created us with minds that could learn from his creation and his acts of providence that he exists and that he is powerful, righteous, just, good, and merciful (Rom. 1:20). God meant for us to see his glory in the world.

God created two families of beings, angelic and human, with minds that could know him and give him glory. And he made two homes, heaven and earth, which are each suited to one of these families of beings. He placed his angels in heaven and us on the earth. God gave us authority to rule over everything on earth. We are a constant declaration of God's image, and his glory, to all creation. Angels have a parallel purpose in heaven: to glorify God.

This creation was, in God's own judgment, "very good" (Gen. 1:31). And one beauty of its original setup was that there was nothing between God and his angels and human beings. Thus, there was no need for a mediator (see Gen. 3:8[1]).

This beautiful order, this union between the two families of God, was shattered by sin. Many angels and all human beings rejected their dependence on God and rebelled against him. Because God was no longer the center of their lives, they began to devour one another in hatred (see the story of Cain and Abel in Genesis 4—as well as the rest of history). God cursed the earth and everything in it. The angels who remained obedient to God stayed in heaven with him, but all humanity was shut out of his glorious presence. He even put cherubim and a flaming

1. Although the meeting in Genesis 3 is clouded by the first sin, God meets directly with Adam and Eve, without a mediator.

sword at the entrance of the garden of Eden in order to keep us out (Gen. 3:24).

God demonstrated his terrifying severity by righteously rejecting the fallen angels forever, but he showed mercy by determining to recover some of mankind. Even as he was rescuing some people, however, he continued to leave them for a time separated from the angels—one family in heaven and another family on earth. But his plan was to bring them together, under a single head, so that these two families of wonderful creatures would make one glorious family. This is what Paul speaks of in Ephesians 1:9–10, quoted at the beginning of this chapter, and he says again in Colossians 1:20 that God was pleased "through [this single head] to reconcile to himself all things, whether on earth or in heaven."

This new head of everything in heaven and on earth is Jesus Christ—the Son of God who was made man (1 Cor. 11:3; Eph. 1:22–23). This glory was reserved for him; no one else was worthy of it.

> And he is before all things, and in him all things hold together. And he is the head of the body, the church. He is the beginning, the firstborn from the dead, that in everything he might be preeminent. For in him all the fullness of God was pleased to dwell. (Col. 1:17–19)

As head of God's restored family, Christ was given all power in heaven and on earth as well as the fullness of grace and glory. We, as well as the angels, get nothing from God except through Christ. In him we live, on him we depend, to him we bow.[2]

Of course, angels and human beings are different, so Christ became the head of each in different ways. The angels who didn't fall into sin didn't need grace and a redeemer as we did. But for

2. See chapter 2.

each one, Christ is the head and brings everything together. This is more than putting the egg back together again. In Christ, everything that is broken will be made whole.

The Glory of Glories

This abridged history of the world barely touches God's mysterious work of wisdom to restore everything through Jesus Christ. But we've seen enough to know that Christ's true glory is light-years beyond what we can imagine. Still, when by faith we reflect on his restoring work, the Spirit can stretch our thoughts; our meditations can catch the coattails of his glory when we think, for example, about things such as the following.

Christ Alone Could Bear the Weight of This Glory

No mere creature, in heaven or on earth, was fit to be head of God's entire creation. No one else could stand in the place of God: Who else could all things depend on? Who else could all things submit to? Who else could be the conduit of all things that come from God to his creatures? So when the Spirit speaks of Christ's glory, he describes him in terms that make clear that there's no one like him.

> He is the radiance of the glory of God and the exact imprint of his nature, and he upholds the universe by the word of his power. (Heb. 1:3)

> He is the image of the invisible God, the firstborn of all creation. For by him all things were created, in heaven and on earth, visible and invisible, whether thrones or dominions or rulers or authorities—all things were created through him and for him. And he is before all things, and in him all things hold together. (Col. 1:15–17)

148

Christ's Glory as Head of All Is His Greatest Glory

God planned for his eternal Son to become man. We know that he did this in order to rescue his people from sin. But now we see that there's more to God's plan: he's not simply going to redeem his people, as wondrous as that is; he's going to bring everything—the whole creation—together in him. He is the fountain of everything and holds it all together forever.

How can I capture in words the divine beauty, order, and harmony of this? Communion between angels and human beings; the shower of life, grace, power, mercy, and consolations to the church; the rule of everything for the glory of God—these all depend on Christ's restoring everything. This is the glory God designed for the Son, and no glory can compare to it.

Since this is his highest glory, reflecting on it should move us with delight and joy. To see Christ in the place of God, as the supreme head of the whole creation, ruling and caring for it, should refresh every believer's soul.

As Ruler of All Creation, Christ Restores the Glory of God That Was Violated by Sin

Have you gasped in awe at a sunrise draped over mist-shrouded mountains? Have you been stopped in your tracks by a forest of towering pines? Have your eyes grown moist with joy at the birth of your first child? These wonders are but shadows and echoes of the glory of the original creation. Everything around us and in us is groaning under the curse of sin (Rom. 8:20–22). The beauty of the first creation sang the being, goodness, wisdom, and eternal power of God. This was all vandalized by sin—more unthinkably than if someone took a machete to the *Mona Lisa*. But when Christ restores everything, he'll make the heavens and the earth even more glorious than they were in the beginning.

This is the glory of Christ.

Christ Is the Only Way We Can Know God's Infinite Wisdom

The wisdom of God is always and in everything infinite. God can't do one thing more wisely than he does another. He wasn't wiser in creating us than he was in making algae. When he first created all things, his unlimited wisdom was united to his unlimited power: "O LORD, how manifold are your works! In wisdom have you made them *all*" (Ps. 104:24). But when the beauty and glory of the first creation were defaced, it took even greater treasures of wisdom to repair the damage. So by putting everything back together in Christ and pouring more glory on it than ever, God is doing the highest thing for his creatures that he'll ever do.

Paul explains that this is the only way we can know the fullness of God's wisdom.

> To me, though I am the very least of all the saints, this grace was given, to preach to the Gentiles the unsearchable riches of Christ, and to bring to light for everyone what is the plan of the mystery hidden for ages in God, who created all things, so that through the church *the manifold wisdom of God might now be made known* to the rulers and authorities in the heavenly places. This was according to the eternal purpose that he has realized in Christ Jesus our Lord. (Eph. 3:8–11)

This is the way that even the angels know the fullness of God's wisdom—they couldn't have known it before sin came into the world, because there was nothing for God to repair. They didn't know there was something beyond the original glory of creation. But in Christ, in this plan to restore all creation, is "hidden all the treasures of wisdom and knowledge" (Col. 2:3). Jesus is eternally glorious in this great work.

Christ Will Keep the New Creation Glorified Forever

As wonderful as the first creation was, it was capable of being ruined. The sin of angels and of human beings scarred and twisted its beauty. But now everything that belongs to this new creation—every believer in the world and every angel in heaven—is secured from ruin. Christ will glorify us and keep us glorified forever.

More Than I Can Ever Say

Who can talk about these things with the words they deserve? Who can describe the glory of Christ? I feel like I've just started. But I hope that now you and I will use these meditations to reflect on his glory through the mirror of the Scriptures, see it with the eyes of our faith, and see it at least clearly enough that we'll admire and adore him every day of our lives.

For Reflection and Discussion

1. Christ is the Bridegroom of the church, his beautiful bride. With this in mind, answer the question that is posed in Song of Songs 5:9: "What is your beloved more than another beloved, O most beautiful among women?"

2. According to this chapter, which glory of Christ is greater than all others? Why?

3. How does Christ's glory in bringing together angels and human beings in one body show God's manifold wisdom?

Christ, We Do All Adore Thee

Christ, we do all adore thee,
and we do praise thee forever;
Christ, we do all adore thee,
and we do praise thee forever;
for on the holy cross
hast thou the world from sin redeemed.
Christ, we do all adore thee,
and we do praise thee forever.
Christ, we do all adore thee.

LATIN HYMN

*We've by no means come to
the end of the glory of Christ,
but it's time to think about what
lies ahead. What we can see of
Christ now by faith, as glorious
as it is, can't begin to compare
with what we'll see in heaven.*

11

to live divided, with but half a heart

. . . . *to live*
Divided, with but half a heart,
Till we shall meet and never part.
—HENRY KING

Exiled

Olomouc lies in the heart of Moravia, three hours east of Prague by train, twenty-four hours away, by planes, trains, and automobiles, from New Mexico, our home in 1996. I counted those hours as I made my way east for a two-month sabbatical that winter. My wife and I tried to bridge the distance between us with love letters that melted the snow around my flat. Her letters to me were my food and drink, the sunshine that pierced the gray winter sky. Every day at noon, I charged up the five flights of stairs to ask the concierge for my mail. When I saw my name formed in my wife's hand on an envelope, I would go straight to my room and devour every line, feasting on our love.

And yet, as delicious as her letters were, they weren't enough. Within the first week of my sabbatical, I began to punctuate my journal entries with groans and sighs. Those groans and sighs grew until the final days, when I wrote, "All I want is to grab her and never let her go." Love letters are no match for the real thing—face to face, warm arms wrapped around warm bodies, staring into your lover's eyes.

The "not enoughness" of love letters is an illustration of how we see Christ by faith in this life. We can bask for hours in his glory as the God-man, or as the only face of God to us, or as the wisdom of God, or as the love of God—and that glory feeds, comforts, and delights our souls. But it isn't enough. There's something more, something we can't have in this life, and it makes us ache to be with him. Lovers of Christ, like David and Paul, experienced his glory and love to the deepest extent they can be known by faith, yet they cried out for more.

> My soul thirsts for God,
>   for the living God.
> When shall I come and appear before God? (Ps. 42:2)

> My desire is to depart and be with Christ, for that is far better. (Phil. 1:23)

What David and Paul felt was the frustration of living by faith and not by sight (2 Cor. 5:7). In this life, we live before God by faith alone. By faith we take part in his grace, holiness, and joy, but someday, by sight, we'll take hold of eternal happiness and glory when we see Christ face to face.

By faith now, and by sight in heaven, we take hold of the same thing: the glory of Christ. By faith we "see" his glory in this life, when we meditate on him as he's revealed to us in the Scriptures. That's what this book is about. But in this chapter we'll explore the difference between the glimpse we have of him in this life and the vision we'll have of him in the next—it's all the difference in the world.

In a Mirror Dimly

Although we've spent most of this book celebrating the joy and comfort and strength we experience when we see Christ's glory as it can be viewed in this world by faith, what we are seeing is an obscure, dark image—like a face reflected in the freshly polished hood of a car. Paul didn't have in mind the refined mirrors of our day when he said, "For now we see *in a mirror dimly*, but then face to face. Now I know in part; then I shall know fully, even as I have been fully known" (1 Cor. 13:12). Face to face is what we long for, but here we see only a reflection—and a dim reflection at that.

We can see Christ in the gospel, and through these past chapters I hope you've seen that he is altogether lovely, the Desired of the nations, the Rose of Sharon, the Morning Star. Yet the image we can perceive by faith, as beautiful as it is to us, is unfocused and incomplete compared to his unclouded glory in heaven.

The word Paul uses in 1 Corinthians 13:12 to describe the view we can have of Christ in this life is the one that gives us our English word *enigma*. An enigma is a riddle or a puzzling saying. This suggests another way that we can think of the difference between seeing Christ by faith and seeing him face to face: A riddle intrigues us because we sense that its solution is graspable but is just beyond us; we understand a little of it, and our minds itch to solve it. Similarly, we see and know Christ a little and also know there is much more of him to know, and thus we itch to know him fully. In the end, we will.

But I should clarify that it isn't the gospel that's dark and obscure—the gospel plainly sets forth Christ as well as his crucifixion, exaltation, and glorification. Paul isn't saying that Christ's revelation to us is obscure; it's the *instrument* by which we receive and comprehend that revelation that is necessarily incomplete for now. We receive it by faith, and since our faith is weak and imperfect, we comprehend Christ's glory that is portrayed through the gospel as people understand a riddle or a parable—imperfectly and with difficulty. Job was feeling this when he said of God, "Behold, these are but the outskirts of his ways, and how small a whisper do we hear of him!" (Job 26:14). We're so weak that we can take in only a bit of his glory—and even when we do take it in, we can't hold it for long. This is the frustration of walking by faith.

Like the frustrated beloved in Solomon's Song, we catch only glimpses of Christ, as if he's behind a wall, or looking through a window, or peering through the lattice (Song 2:9); our view of him is blocked or patchy or unstable. The weakness of our sinful flesh is the wall between us and our Beloved, and it has to be destroyed before we can see him face to face. But sometimes he looks through the window or the lattice of the gospel, and we get a refreshing glimpse of him. Still, it's not enough, and we cry with David,

> As a deer pants for flowing streams,
>   so pants my soul for you, O God.
> My soul thirsts for God,
>   for the living God.
> When shall I come and appear before God? (Ps. 42:1–2)

Face to Face, with New Eyes

Things are going to change. Someday we'll look on Christ with a steady, fixed gaze. Instead of seeing a reflected image of him in the gospel, we'll see him "face to face," which Paul contrasts with the "enigmatic" reflection we see of him now

(1 Cor. 13:12). We'll see him as he is (1 John 3:2), not his partial portrait. We won't even be limited to just a brief glimpse of his back as he passes in front of us (Ex. 33:21–23); we'll see him and talk with him as you might talk with your neighbor in front of your house.

And we'll see him with the eyes in our heads—it won't be some "spiritual apprehension":

> For I know that my Redeemer lives,
>   and at the last he will stand upon the earth.
> And after my skin has been thus destroyed,
>   yet in my flesh I shall see God,
> whom I shall see for myself,
>   and my eyes shall behold, and not another.
>   My heart faints within me! (Job 19:25–27)

God will restore and glorify our eyes in heaven so we can out-see the eagle. And he'll do this for one reason: to answer our Lord's prayer in John 17:24 so we can eternally drink in the Lamb and his glory. With the very eyes that we now use to see the tokens of Christ in the bread and wine of Communion, we'll one day see him in the flesh. Doesn't that quicken your pulse?

And we won't just see Christ's human nature. We'll see his divine person in union with his human nature. We'll see the perfection of infinite wisdom, love, and power in him. All the glories of Christ that we have so weakly and faintly seen reflected in this life will fill our eyes forever.

To be face to face with Christ is what we pine for. We want, like Paul, "to depart and be with Christ, for that is far better" (Phil. 1:23). We would rather "be away from the body and at home with the Lord" (2 Cor. 5:8), where we'll enjoy the sight of the Lamb in his glory for which we have waited with inexpressible longing.

To be able to see Christ in glory, we'll have to be changed. "Beloved, we are God's children now, and what we will be has not yet appeared" (1 John 3:2). Until we are changed, we can't see him as he is. When he was transfigured and his human nature was clothed with some reflections of his divine glory, his disciples weren't refreshed by it; instead, "they fell on their faces and were terrified" (Matt. 17:6). They saw his glory, but when Peter started talking about it, "he did not know what he was saying" (Luke 9:33 NIV). The reason was that no one in this life has the eyes—either spiritual or physical—to see and apprehend the glory of Christ face to face.

In fact, if the Lord Jesus walked up beside you now in his majesty and glory and tapped you on the shoulder, it wouldn't comfort you. You aren't fit or ready to bear his full glory. His beloved apostle John had leaned against him many times as his dear friend, but when Jesus appeared to him in his glory, John "fell at his feet as though dead" (Rev. 1:17). And when Jesus appeared to Paul, all that Paul could say about it was that he saw "a light from heaven, brighter than the sun," and that he and his companions fell to the ground (Acts 26:13–14). This was one reason why during his ministry here on earth, Christ cloaked his glory under the weakness of flesh and suffering—to spare us from seeing his glory before we were ready.

For now, we are fit to know the Son only by the Spirit. We no longer know him through the physical means of the worship ceremonies of the Old Testament; we're beyond that. And we don't know him by his bodily presence as his disciples did in Galilee twenty centuries ago; we're beyond that too. We sometimes wish that we could see him in his flesh as the disciples did then, but Jesus himself said that what we have now is better by far: "Nevertheless, I tell you the truth: it is to your advantage that I go away, for if I do not go away, the Helper will not come to you. But if I go, I will send him to you" (John 16:7). The view that we have of his glory now by faith is better than what they had of his humanity with their eyes. Still, it isn't enough.

A New Mind

For us to see the Lamb in all his glory, our minds will have to be overhauled. God will literally change our minds. He'll drive away their last shadow of ignorance, firm up their slightest unsteadiness, remove every obstruction that has ever hindered or blocked or blurred our sight of Christ.

Our flesh makes our minds vain, dark, corrupt—unable to discern anything spiritual (1 Cor. 2:14). When we're born again into the kingdom at conversion, God heals the darkness of original sin that blinded us so that we can see truly, but that healing isn't finished. We're like the blind man whom Jesus healed in two stages: instead of being blind as a bat he was able to see men walking around, but they looked like trees; once Jesus touched him a second time, everything was crystal clear (Mark 8:22–25). So we can see spiritual things and discern spiritual truth and even take hold of Christ by faith, but we're still frustrated by error and weakness—we groan for that final healing touch. When he reaches out his hand again, he won't leave the least trace of a scar or wound (Eph. 5:27).

Try to imagine how precious this will be. Today our minds are slow to pray. When we finally turn our thoughts to spiritual things, we can hardly stay focused for two minutes before our minds flit to the ephemera of everyday life: a word from a friend that stung, an overdue assignment we keep putting off, something we forgot to get at the store. But when our minds are made new, nothing will be able to wrest our eyes from Christ and his glory. We won't grow tired or bored. We won't be tempted to look for something more interesting to do. Our thoughts will be honey from the comb. And just one such thought of the Lamb will fill us with more satisfaction and pleasure than all our best thoughts in this world rolled together.

A New Body

When our bodies are glorified, we'll see our Redeemer with our eyes (Job 19:25–27). We don't yet know how our bodies will be changed (1 Cor. 15:35–49), but God will make them ready to bear and enjoy eternal happiness in his presence.

The first Christian martyr, Stephen, tasted some of this glory before he died. When he was brought to trial before the council, "gazing at him, all who sat in the council saw that his face was like the face of an angel" (Acts 6:15). He was transfigured to some degree, not unlike Jesus in Matthew 17. And the beginning of his glorification caused his eyes to grow so keen and powerful that he stared through the inconceivable distance between earth and heaven and "saw the glory of God, and Jesus standing at the right hand of God" (Acts 7:55). Who, then, can say what will be the power of our sense of sight, when it is glorified, or what sweetness and refreshment we'll take in through our renewed eyes?

If you could travel back to any time in history and any place on the planet, when and where would you go? My father and I used to play this game. He'd talk about wanting to see King Arthur in Camelot but would always come back to Jesus—he wanted to see Jesus in the flesh. Who of us wouldn't give the world for such a chance? And when the disciples saw our Lord in his body, they saw what "many prophets and righteous people longed to see" (Matt. 13:17). As remarkable as that privilege was, it's small when compared to what Stephen saw when he peered into heaven to see the Lord Jesus in his uncloaked glory. So how wonderful will it be, then, when our eyes are gloriously purified and strengthened beyond Stephen's?

This Present Darkness

This glorious vision is what we pant after as the deer pants for water (Ps. 42:1). It's the answer to our Lord's dying prayer (John 17:24) and the ultimate satisfaction for our souls. How is it different from the glorious glimpses of Christ that we gain by faith now?

Here on earth, we're loaded down with the burden of our weakness. Our remaining ignorance and frailty handicap our faith. Even in those best moments, when heaven seems to break through and we adore and admire our glorious Christ, filled with wonder at his beauty, seemingly transported to heaven by his gentle and courageous love for us—even then our worship is punctuated with our groans for deliverance.

> And not only the creation, but we ourselves, who have the firstfruits of the Spirit, groan inwardly as we wait eagerly for adoption as sons, the redemption of our bodies. For in this hope we were saved. Now hope that is seen is not hope. For who hopes for what he sees? (Rom. 8:23–24)

As we grow in faith and spiritual understanding, we grow more aware of our burdens, and we more urgently groan for deliverance—for the perfect freedom of the sons of God. This is a mark of those who are mature in the Spirit. The nearer we are to heaven, the more we long to be there, because Christ is there. The more frequently and steadily we see him by faith, the more we long and groan for the obliteration of every obstruction that clouds our view of him.

In fact, we can't think of Christ without being ashamed of and troubled by our own thoughts—they seem so confused, unsteady, and imperfect. We groan that we can't think better about him, can't think longer about him, aren't moved more

163

deeply by him. Oh! when will we come to him? When will we be with him and not have to leave? When will we see him as he is? Usually this trouble and groaning follows or even fills our best meditations—a trouble that I ask God never to deliver me from before I die.

Believers' hearts that are moved by the glory of Christ are like compass needles that can't fix on the pole. Our hearts can't be still; they can no longer be satisfied to be away from Jesus. Our hearts pant and sigh and groan and weep as we pray and meditate. They continually turn toward Christ, their pole, but never quite come to rest.

A Cloud of Witnesses

We saw in chapter 8 that Old Testament believers received precious revelations of the glory of Christ; however, they were obscure and incomplete compared to the revelation we now cherish in the finished Scriptures. Old Testament believers could see Christ—but only under the cloak of shadows and types and symbols and metaphors. Still, it was the food of their faith, and they "searched and inquired carefully" to find what the Spirit had to say about Christ (1 Peter 1:10–11). Their example teaches us to search out the glory of Christ while we are still struggling against ignorance and weakness.

They had great spiritual wisdom. They rejoiced and gloried in the ceremonies of worship. They looked on them as their highest privilege and gave their hearts to them because they were the designs of divine wisdom and love and a shadow of good things ahead. But at the same time, they longed for the restoration to come, when they would see and enjoy the wonders that were symbolized by their worship. And those who didn't look forward, who rested and trusted in the shadows themselves, were rejected by God.

Don't you admire Moses and Ruth and David and Isaiah? Think of how dark some of the Old Testament seems to you now, even though you have the gospel to explain it and the Spirit to lift the veil. How much more mysterious it must have been to them, yet they saw "the things promised . . . and welcomed them from a distance" (Heb. 11:13 NIV). They reached out their arms, in their most ardent affection, to embrace what was promised. And when one of the last of them took the child Jesus in his arms, he cried out to God, "Now dismiss your servant in peace" (Luke 2:28 NIV), as if to say, "I can die now; I've seen what my soul has always longed for."

The darkness and weakness we experience isn't like theirs. Our darkness comes from the nature of faith itself and the fact that we are seeing Christ's reflected image in the gospel rather than seeing him face to face. But the vision of the Lamb that we'll enjoy in heaven is immeasurably clearer and greater than what we have now—so much so that the difference between the way we see Christ by faith and the way Old Testament believers saw him is almost nothing in comparison. So if they prayed and yearned to see what we see, how much more should we ache for our faith to become sight?

At Home in Exile?

Suppose that, while on my sabbatical in Central Europe, I had written this to my bride:

My dearest Paula,
Your letters are my delight—they fill me with innumerable pleasures! I've grown so fond of them that I've decided to stay here in Olomouc, away from you, so that I can always enjoy them.
Your beloved husband

Whatever I might have intended by sending such a letter, it would not have been read with pleasure. It would have exposed a pathology in my love for her. Similarly, although we revel in the sight of Christ that our faith now offers us, if we don't long for the perfect view of him that we will have in heaven but are satisfied to leave things as they are now, our love for him is ailing. Until we're perfected, weakness and disease are a perennial threat to our communion with Christ. Therefore, we regularly check our hearts and seek the Spirit's healing and renewal. This is exactly what we will do in our last two chapters.

For Reflection and Discussion

1. Christ is the Bridegroom of the church, his beautiful bride. With this in mind, answer the question that is posed in Song of Songs 5:9: "What is your beloved more than another beloved, O most beautiful among women?"

2. What does it mean that we see the glory of Christ only "in a mirror dimly" (1 Cor. 13:12) during this life?

3. What kinds of things make the view of his glory that we can have in this life clearer? Less clear?

4. What can you do in order to gain a clearer view of Christ by faith?

5. Can you think of a time when you've been overwhelmed by a yearning to be with Christ face to face? Describe it. If you've not experienced such a yearning, why not?

6. What is one thing about seeing Christ face to face that you look forward to?

A long hike sometimes shows us that we're out of shape. Maybe all this talk of longing for Christ has made you realize that your heart isn't in the right place. Let's ask ourselves some hard questions.

12

my heart within me like a stone

The truth is, I haven't any language weak enough to depict the weakness of my spiritual life. If I weakened it enough it would cease to be language at all. Like when you try to turn the gas-ring a little lower still, and it merely goes out.
—C. S. Lewis

Aging Gracefully

Believers who are close to leaving this world have a two-sided longing. One side is a longing to recover from any spiritual decay or backsliding that has hung about us like a ball and chain; the other is a longing to be spiritually refreshed, so that we are more spiritually minded and can grow in holiness and bear fruit for the kingdom. We treasure the two sides of this coin more than the world and everything in it. Our sights are locked on these.

Refreshing grace is the only thing that can buoy us up through all the troubles and temptations that face us at the end

169

of our lives' journey. Paul says that spiritual renewal kept him from losing heart as he saw his earthly life fading: "Though our outer self is wasting away, our inner self is being renewed day by day" (2 Cor. 4:16). Troubles, especially near life's end, will overwhelm us if our hearts aren't continually renewed and revived, because hardships increase with age: friends die, hips break, eyes cloud over, regrets fester, and fond memories fade, until we may even wish with Job that God would put us out of our misery (Job 6:8–9). The only thing that can rescue us from a death wish is the daily spiritual renovation of our inner lives.

Would it surprise you to find out that God promises to renew his gray-headed saints? The psalmist declares God's mercy to them.

> The righteous flourish like the palm tree
>   and grow like a cedar in Lebanon.
> They are planted in the house of the LORD;
>   they flourish in the courts of our God.
> *They still bear fruit in old age;*
>   *they are ever full of sap and green,*
> to declare that the LORD is upright;
>   he is my rock, and there is no unrighteousness in him.
>   (Ps. 92:12–15)

This promise echoes the waterfall of blessings we find in Psalm 72 that celebrate the days of the Messiah: "In his days may the righteous flourish" (v. 7). It's the hope of the grace that will overflow from Christ's fullness (see John 1:16; Col. 1:19). This inward flourishing of God's people glorifies our Messiah. When believers are dry stumps and lifeless stones, the church has no glory—no matter how beautiful its ceremonies or how much it outwardly prospers. The glory of kings is the wealth and peace of their subjects; the glory of Christ is the grace and holiness of his.

The psalmist says this flourishing is like the palm tree and its growth like the cedar. The palm tree is known for its lush beauty and fruitfulness, and the cedar is renowned for its towering height. So the children of the kingdom are known for the beauty of their faith and the fruitfulness of their obedience, as well as for their constant growth and increase in grace. And this is true for all believers, unless by our own sinful neglect we stunt our growth and become scrub oak.

But the key words of Psalm 92 are in verse 14, which we quoted above: "They still bear fruit *in old age*; they are ever full of sap and green." God reverses the course of nature. Aging believers will be fresh and "full of sap," green and bearing fruit. Their freshness will come from the sap of grace that continually flows from Christ himself—the vine from whom they draw the life of God (John 15:1–8). They will be green and vigorous, not withered and brittle. To their last days, their boughs will be heavy with the fruit of love and obedience.

This is God's promise. Although we face natural decay and, at times, spiritual decay, he has provided in his covenant a way to make us fresh, green, and fruitful. This *unnatural* privilege enables us, even when we are weak, to declare, "The Lord is upright; he is my rock, and there is no unrighteousness in him" (Ps. 92:15).

Think about the burdens of old age: the frustration of forgetting things, or waking up every day in pain, or depending on someone else to bathe and dress you, or being cut off from family and friends in a nursing home. When the faith of such believers is fresh and green and flourishing, there is no natural way to account for it; it is the faithfulness and power of our God.

The Prosperity Gospel

The spiritual life that God gives us in Christ will increase and flourish until the end. That's one way to tell the difference between true faith and temporary faith. Both may look strong at first, but temporary faith will eventually wither (Matt. 13:20–21). So when our spiritual lives are flat or in decline for a long time, we should be alarmed; we should search our hearts and ask the Spirit to show us the true nature of our faith (2 Cor. 13:5).

Such an examination sounds intimidating, but it can be our Lord's means for us to restore hope. When we are spiritually dull for a long time, we think we'll never again grow the way we did when we first came to Christ. But the Spirit can turn us back to what God says and can renew and refresh us as we repent.

God Compares Our Spiritual Lives to Objects That Can't *Not* Grow

God calls true believers trees that are planted in good soil and watered well (Ps. 1:3). He also says they're like the sun, which is faint at dawn but "shines brighter and brighter until full day" (Prov. 4:18). So the nature of true faith is to increase. But when our faith is weak or stagnant, we look no different from the hypocrite. The Scriptures don't offer us the "rest" of spiritual decay; they deny us any confidence that we'll see God in heaven after living indifferently to him. On the contrary, the Lamb of God himself threatens cold hearts.

> I know your works. You have the reputation of being alive, but you are dead. Wake up, and strengthen what remains and is about to die, for I have not found your works complete in the sight of my God. Remember, then, what you received and heard. Keep it, and repent. If you will not wake up, I will come like a thief, and you will not know at what hour I will come against you. (Rev. 3:1–3)

> I know your works: you are neither cold nor hot. Would that you were either cold or hot! So, because you are lukewarm,

and neither hot nor cold, I will spit you out of my mouth. For you say, I am rich, I have prospered, and I need nothing, not realizing that you are wretched, pitiable, poor, blind, and naked. I counsel you to buy from me gold refined by fire, so that you may be rich, and white garments so that you may clothe yourself and the shame of your nakedness may not be seen, and salve to anoint your eyes, so that you may see. Those whom I love, I reprove and discipline, so be zealous and repent. (Rev. 3:15–19)

Of course, even true believers sometimes stray, sometimes linger under clouds of sin and trials. But they're like the sun that is hidden behind the clouds of the storm for a while but later breaks out with more glory than before.

God Promises to Give Us the Grace We Need to Flourish Right to the End

God's promises create and maintain our spiritual lives. Through them, we take part in his nature (2 Peter 1:4). Consider one such promise:

> For I will pour water on the thirsty land,
>   and streams on the dry ground;
> I will pour my Spirit upon your offspring,
>   and my blessing on your descendants.
> They shall spring up among the grass
>   like willows by flowing streams. (Isa. 44:3–4)

When we study the context of this promise, we discover that God is telling Israel about the myriad blessings waiting for them when they return from their exile in Babylon. But the New Testament makes it clear that these restoration promises are fulfilled in Christ to the new Israel, the Israel that is by faith.

This promise teaches us what we are in ourselves, both before and after our conversion: thirsty, dry, and barren ground. In ourselves, we don't have one drop of water or one sunbeam to turn us green or make our branches bend with fruit (2 Cor. 3:5). Left to ourselves, we parch and crack like west Texas ten years into a drought.

But God comes to us in Christ to pour the sanctifying water of his Spirit on us. And we'll green up like grass after rain and grow tall like the cottonwoods that line the Rio Grande. You can spot those cottonwoods from miles around—nothing else in the desert grows as tall. That's how we'll grow as we feed on these promises (Ps. 1:3). But to feed on his promises correctly, we need to know that God expects us to *take hold* of them.

Unlike trees and grass, we can't just sit and wait for God to rain his blessings on us. We're bound by his covenant to many duties through which he fulfills these promises to us (2 Peter 1:4–10). This is the ordinary way we receive the grace that makes us flourish—by diligently obeying God, by faith, as we depend on the Holy Spirit. Sometimes God surprises us with healing grace while we are backsliding (see Isa. 57:17–18), and the Good Shepherd in his sovereign mercy will go out of his way to retrieve a wandering sheep, but the ordinary way that we grow is by working out our faith with fear and trembling.

And that means that *in spite of these glorious promises, our negligence can render us spiritually weak and barren.* This is why we see such a discrepancy between the gospel's promises about the glory and beauty of the church, and the lives of many Christians. God has promised us countless times that our spiritual lives will thrive, grow, and flourish, even in old age and up to death's door, but we won't be refreshed while we're asleep in spiritual sloth.

Think of it this way: life must be preserved by food, and God has provided the food for our spiritual lives. This food is the Word of God.

Like newborn infants, long for the pure spiritual milk, that by it you may grow up into salvation—if indeed you have tasted that the Lord is good. (1 Peter 2:2–3)

God has served up a great feast in his Word. But if we refuse to eat, it's no wonder that we shrivel like spiritual raisins. If we're unwilling to dig into his Word, or if we think so little of his Word that we ignore it, how can we help but die on the vine? But God has provided all the nourishment we need, even to our last days.

The Painful Reality

Despite God's promises that we will thrive, and the gracious provisions he has made for our growth, we sometimes wither. And those who have believed the longest are often the most susceptible to even the kind of spiritual decay that fills us with confusion, doubt, and fear for the eternal safety of our souls.

Spiritual decay can be a slippery slope or a sheer cliff. The slippery slope is a gradual and general decline that drains vigor from our spiritual lives. The sheer cliff is a sudden, overwhelming temptation that leads to a fall into sin—the kind of sin that wastes our consciences and robs us of peace.

Temporary believers eventually show their true colors—especially if, in God's providence, they face either unusual prosperity or hardship. They may hang on to the outward trappings of Christianity, but their lives will demonstrate nothing of God's power to make them new (Prov. 1:31; 2 Tim. 3:5).

Temporary believers don't realize that they're growing cold. Their minds are full of everything but Christ, and their eyes are fixed on earthly things, so they never see how unfruitful they are. Or, if they do sense a change, they don't care; they are like the sluggards who moan, "A little sleep, a little slumber, a little folding of the hands to rest" (Prov. 6:10). But believers are restless backsliders; they are never happy to be far from God. The chill in our souls pricks our hearts. Even when we fall into Satan's traps or when our own flesh fools us—or when we're just plain ignorant of how we can recover from spiritual decay—even then our hearts can't sit still.

The Scriptures show us many examples of those who slide down the slippery slope or drop off the sheer cliff. The Lord Christ accuses five of the seven churches whom he addresses in Revelation 2 and 3 of slowly rotting. Some of those Christians, and especially those at Sardis and Laodicea, had fallen so far that they were in danger of Christ's judgment: he threatened to remove their lampstand from its place. Perhaps you've seen this in your life—a casual drifting away from God until you hardly know him. *Holy Father, please keep us from drifting!*

And don't we grieve over the long list of believers, many of them are among the greatest followers of Christ, who inexplicably dive into some sin that wrecks their consciences? Our hearts break for David as he trembles under the weight of his sin.

> O LORD, rebuke me not in your anger,
>   nor discipline me in your wrath!
> For your arrows have sunk into me,
>   and your hand has come down on me.
>
> There is no soundness in my flesh
>   because of your indignation;
> there is no health in my bones
>   because of my sin.
>
> For my iniquities have gone over my head;
>   like a heavy burden, they are too heavy for me.
>
> My wounds stink and fester
>   because of my foolishness. (Ps. 38:1–5)

When we're overcome by a grave sin or through carelessness continue in evil for a long time, we know God's displeasure—we can't mistake his frown. Fear opens our minds and hearts and shows us how sick we are. Not everyone feels it as sharply as David did in Psalm 38, since his fall was great, but we feel it nonetheless. And each heart knows its own bitterness (Prov. 14:10).

Under such conviction, we feel alone. Our hearts suffer for days on end, and others can't understand why we aren't happy. But it's better to see believers grieving over their backsliding than to see them indifferently falling away from God. The sad ones—those who feel the weight of their sin—are on the road to recovery; the ones who are unbothered are on the road that leads to death.

Search Me, O God

It's hard for people to be convinced of their spiritual decay—and recovery is even harder. But without the convincing, there can't be any healing. This convincing is the work of the Spirit (Ps. 139:23–24), and we should seek his conviction. So pause now and ask him to help you through the next few pages, and see whether he'll uncover any dullness in your heart regarding Christ.

Have Your Fervent Love for Christ and Faithfulness to Him Diminished?

Almost every life that the Old Testament records for us to learn from is the life of someone who fell and then found help from God. Remember David's lament in Psalm 38? In Psalm 103, he celebrates his deliverance.

Bless the LORD, O my soul,
and forget not all his benefits,

who forgives all your iniquity,
    who heals all your diseases,
who redeems your life from the pit,
    who crowns you with steadfast love and mercy,
who satisfies you with good
    so that your youth is renewed like the eagle's. (Ps. 103:2–5)

What kindness of God is more precious to us than his healing our spiritual sickness and restoring our spiritual strength?

Since God so often warns us about spiritual decay, and since he so often promises that we will be recovered from it, and since we have so many striking examples in the Bible of people who stumbled, it shouldn't surprise us that there are many in the church whose hearts are dull. But what about you? How is it with your soul? Are you drifting away from Christ?

Do You Still Have Peace and Joy?

Peace and joy come from a healthy life of faith. Have your peace and joy stayed with you through hardships and temptation, or do you quickly become uneasy and confused? The peace of Christ isn't consistent with spiritual decay. When we've lost our peace, we know that we have in some degree slipped away from Christ.

Do You See Outward Signs of Decay in Your Spiritual Life?

Often we don't need to mine deep within our souls to find rot. It's lying right on the surface where anyone can see it, like paint peeling off the walls. Arrogance, selfishness, extravagant spending, devotion to diversions, loose talk, obsessive work or ambition: These are the ways of the world. They are not the ways of Enoch and Abraham and Moses and David and Isaiah and Paul and John, who lived to please their Lord. And is this how we lived when we first came to Christ (Jer. 2:2)? If you feel the pricking of conviction in your heart, call on the Lamb to heal you.

Are You Tired of God?

The very question shocks us, but it can happen. We're tired of God when we lose our taste for public worship or for private devotions, when we avoid family prayer—or, worse, when we're outwardly faithful in our spiritual duties but are hiding an inward robotic lifelessness, drawing close to God with our lips while our hearts are away from him (Isa. 29:13; Matt. 15:8; Mark 7:6). I say this is worse because "God is spirit, and those who worship him must worship in spirit and truth" (John 4:24), and because God makes such sobering threats to those whose worship is hollow (see Ps. 50). God won't be mocked.

It isn't easy to keep our minds fit for worship. It demands spiritual diligence and watchfulness, as Jesus told his drowsy disciples in the garden (Matt. 26:41). The world, the flesh, and the devil all oppose us and want to make us into latter-day Pharisees. They use temptations to be morally careless, or worldly, or just plain lazy to lull our spirits to sleep in a field of poppies when the Emerald City lies in sight. Our flesh will try to get us to rest on our spiritual laurels, a temptation for those who have long served God. To stay a step ahead of this inward persecutor, we must strive to lay hold of God (Isa. 64:7)—and constantly striving to lay hold of him is a sign of robust spiritual health.

Another way we can dull our hearts and make them unfit for worship is by trying to keep hold of a pet sin, as when Augustine prayed for God to give him sexual purity—but not yet. Worshipping in spirit and truth has a great power to destroy sin. No one can worship God in spirit and truth without being broken over their known sins. In order to maintain both secret sin and public worship, we must hollow out our worship until it's an empty shell of formalities.

Does the Glory of God Shine through You?

There are graces that obviously show God's glory—such as zeal for Christ, humility before God and others, brokenness over sin, a mind that is constantly on the things of God, love, and self-denial. Are these coursing through our veins? Are they increasing as we age (2 Peter 1:8) and, through their fruit, showing God's faithful supply of grace? Here are some ways to take measure of our hearts.

How's our spiritual appetite? Do we still relish the milk of the Word of God (1 Peter 2:2–3)? I've known people—especially those who were older—who were hospitalized because they wouldn't eat; something made them lose their taste for food. Someone with no spiritual appetite is just as sick. And we should ask ourselves not only whether we still hunger to hear the Word preached but also why. Motives are hard to expose, but God warned Ezekiel about those who made his preaching the talk of the town: they thought of him as an entertainer and had no interest in obeying the Word (Ezek. 33:30–33). Paul warned Timothy that some people have "itching ears"—they want to hear preaching but not preaching that calls them to repentance (2 Tim. 4:3).

When people get older, they often don't want to eat as much as they used to. Food loses its appeal. It might be tempting for them to think that the food isn't as tasty as it used to be, but the change is in them. In the same way, if we think that preaching isn't as good as it used to be when we were younger, might the change be in our hearts?

Another reason we lose our appetites is that we're stuffed. The sight of a double-fudge brownie can turn our stomachs after we've downed the Mexican combination plate with extra sopapillas. "One who is full loathes honey, but to one who is hungry everything bitter is sweet" (Prov. 27:7). Loss of spiritual appetite can come from being stuffed—stuffed full of self, full of the world.

But those who crave the Word find it sweet (Ps. 19:10)—so much that even its bitterest reproofs are sweet to them.

Is Christ the first and best thought of our lives? When our spirits flourish, everything else in life takes a back seat to the precious Lamb of God. He sits on the throne of all we think about, long for, and do. We want to know and do what pleases him (Eph. 5:10). But backsliders put religion in its place. Faith is just one of many pursuits in their lives. God is an unwelcome intruder into their business, school, friendships, and entertainment.

Do we go out of our way for Christ and his people? Someone who is living in Christ bears fruit—and especially the fruit of love that serves others (John 13; 14; 15:1–17). When God calls us to serve, how quickly do we lift our hands? Reluctance to serve is a sign of spiritual disease.

The Tears of Repentance Will Water Renewal

Few people enjoy thinking and praying through a long list of diagnostic questions like this. But is the Spirit convicting you? Is his light exposing hidden corners where your heart is cold or dark or dry? If so, and if your heart is softening toward Christ and longing for renewal, then rejoice! This is a sign of his grace. And pray. If you're exhausted and can find no words, try those of Christina Rossetti on the following page.

A Better Resurrection

I have no wit, no words, no tears;
    My heart within me like a stone
Is numb'd too much for hopes or fears;
    Look right, look left, I dwell alone;
I lift mine eyes, but dimm'd with grief
    No everlasting hills I see;
My life is in the falling leaf:
    O Jesus, quicken me.

My life is like a faded leaf,
    My harvest dwindled to a husk:
Truly my life is void and brief
    And tedious in the barren dusk;
My life is like a frozen thing,
    No bud nor greenness can I see:
Yet rise it shall—the sap of Spring;
    O Jesus, rise in me.

My life is like a broken bowl,
    A broken bowl that cannot hold
One drop of water for my soul
    Or cordial in the searching cold;
Cast in the fire the perish'd thing;
    Melt and remould it, till it be
A royal cup for Him, my King:
    O Jesus, drink of me.

CHRISTINA ROSSETTI

For Reflection and Discussion

1. One sign of spiritual health is that the Lamb and his Word are more precious to us than anything else. Work through Psalm 119 and see how many ways the psalmist expresses his delight in God's Word. Can you identify twenty?

2. Think about a time of spiritual decay in your life. Do you remember what brought it on? Was it a slippery slope or a sheer cliff? How did you know you were slipping? What are some ways you can guard against a return to that desert?

3. Think of a time when God kept his covenant and restored you again after you had backslidden. How did he rescue you? Write a brief prayer of praise to him that incorporates details of the work he did to restore you.

Finally, to all who
have slipped from the path,
God reaches down his
strong hand to help.

13

parched and ravenous
i seek him

When I deserved it least, God gave me most.
I think it was the Savior's face itself I saw.
—FREDERICK BUECHNER

Babette's Feast

Isak Dinesen's short story "Babette's Feast" tells of a pietistic sect in Norway that was started by a prophet called the Dean. The little community of believers thrived during the Dean's lifetime, but in the years after his death the group dwindles, and those who remain have become "somewhat querulous and quarrelsome, so that sad little schisms would arise in the congregation."[1] Martine and Philippa, the Dean's two daughters, do their best to keep the brothers and sisters together, but these are clearly disciples in decay.

But then Babette wins the French lottery.

1. Isak Dinesen, "Babette's Feast," in *Anecdotes of Destiny* (New York: Random House, 1958), 23–24.

Babette is the maid and cook who has humbly served Martine and Philippa for years and who conceals a secret past: no one knows that she was once a great chef at the Café Anglais in Paris, a chef who could turn a dinner into "a kind of love affair."[2] Because Babette no longer has a family in Paris to return to, she decides to spend every franc of her winnings on one meal for the remaining members of the congregation.

For these simple folk, Babette recreates one of her renowned masterpieces: "Cailles en Sarcophage." She orders a sea turtle and makes turtle soup. She serves the finest Amontillado and follows it with a Veuve Cliquot 1860. She lays before them quails and pastries and fresh fruits. It is glorious.

Something happens during the meal. "The eldest member of the congregation said grace in the Dean's own words. . . . An old brother told the story of his first meeting with the Dean. Another went through that sermon which sixty years ago had brought about his conversion. . . . A sister on the other side of the table opened on the subject of strange happenings which had taken place while the Dean was still amongst his children, and which one might venture to call miracles."[3]

As they reflect on the life and teachings of the Dean and feast on Babette's grace, "Taciturn old people received the gift of tongues; ears that for years had been almost deaf were opened to it. Time itself had merged into eternity. Long after midnight the windows of the house shone like gold, and golden song flowed out into the winter air." Long-broken friendships are mended with warm embraces, and bursts of laughter take the place of deep-rooted grudges. As the narrator puts it, "They had been given one hour of the millennium."[4]

Even in their dying years, these old believers are restored.

2. Dinesen, 58.
3. Dinesen, 55–56.
4. Dinesen, 61–62.

parched and ravenous i seek him

What's told here so well in fiction delightfully portrays what God declares to be possible for his backsliding people.

There's Hope Ahead

If God marked all our slips and stumbles, "O Lord, who could stand?" (Ps. 130:3). If we didn't have help for our failures *every day*, we'd be in a spiritual free fall. Yet as we have seen, God intends for us not to just hang on by our fingernails until the end but to thrive in him. He's provided everything we need to recover from spiritual decay and grow in Christ—even to the very end of our days on earth. In the previous chapter, we looked at a few of the promises he has made about reviving us, but there are more where those came from. There is hope in Christ, a hope that won't disappoint us (Rom. 5:5).

There's Hard Work Ahead

Spiritual recovery is hard work. Yes, all the praise for any health or growth or strength we experience is due to God alone: "Not to us, O Lord, not to us but to your name be the glory, because of your love and faithfulness" (Ps. 115:1). But as we saw in chapter 12, God works through ordinary means, and the ordinary way in which we recover is through the demanding work of killing our flesh. "For if you live according to the flesh you will die, but if by the Spirit you put to death the deeds of the body, you will live" (Rom. 8:13). It's beyond the scope of this book to cover the details of how to defeat the flesh,[5] but I'll offer two warnings about it.

5. As I mentioned in chapter 3, John Owen provides detailed help for our struggle against the flesh in *Of the Mortification of Sin in Believers*, reprinted in *The Works of John Owen*, ed. William H. Goold, vol. 6 (Edinburgh: Johnstone & Hunter, 1851; repr., Banner of Truth Trust, 1991). If you don't have the patience to work through his challenging prose, I've adapted Owen's works on sin in *The*

We Must Attack the Flesh with God's Weapons and Not Our Own

Many teachers propose remedies for sin that don't come from God. When we try to offer them to God, he says to us, "Who has asked this of you?" (Isa. 1:12 NIV). The Pharisees, for example, piled high the works and duties that they said would win God's acceptance, yet few of those works came from God's Word. And the church has also developed its share of extrabiblical disciplines and denials. Paul's condemnation of these is final.

These are all destined to perish with use, because they are based on human commands and teachings. Such regulations indeed have an appearance of wisdom, with their self-imposed worship, their false humility and their harsh treatment of the body, but they lack any value in restraining sensual indulgence. (Col. 2:22–23 NIV)

The problem is that we naturally run to man-made solutions. When we're convinced that we're backsliders, we feel the guilt of sin and want relief for our consciences. So we look for a way to turn away God's displeasure—and if we aren't guided by the gospel, our flesh will make two kinds of suggestions. The first will involve some extraordinary duty or service that God has never asked of us; the second will be a multiplication of duties beyond what God commands. Both are condemned by Micah:

With what shall I come before the LORD,
  and bow myself before God on high?
Shall I come before him with burnt offerings,
  with calves a year old?

Enemy Within: Straight Talk about the Power and Defeat of Sin, rev. ed. (Phillipsburg, NJ: P&R Publishing, 2023). My work isn't comprehensive, but it covers his best points in simpler language.

> *Will the* Lord *be pleased with thousands of rams,*
>   *with ten thousands of rivers of oil?*
> *Shall I give my firstborn for my transgression,*
>   *the fruit of my body for the sin of my soul?* (Mic. 6:6–7)

Sometimes our guilt hurts so much that we desperately want to do something extraordinary to stop the pain. But what does God require of us for our spiritual recovery? Renewed obedience to *his* means of killing the flesh. His means are familiar: regularly reading and meditating on his Word[6] and hearing it preached; praying fervently; careful watching against temptation; and fixing our minds on things above, where Christ is seated at the right hand of God.

We Must Attack the Flesh by the Power of the Spirit and in Dependence on Christ

The Spirit rejects self-confidence and independence, and we'll never prosper by trying to obey God's commands in our own strength (2 Cor. 3:5; 9:8)—that's not gospel obedience. Too many people pray and read and fast and give to the poor and struggle to resist temptation through mere self-control, which is as effective as a flyswatter against a grizzly.

Mere self-control leaves Christ out of the picture and leaves us floundering. But listen to our Lord: "If you will diligently listen to the voice of the Lord your God, and do that which is right in his eyes, and give ear to his commandments and keep all his statutes, I will put none of the diseases on you that I put on the Egyptians, for *I am the* Lord, *your healer*" (Ex. 15:26). When we attack the flesh in our own strength, any "success" that we appear to experience can actually be an enemy, if it causes us to let our pride rest self-satisfied, because this leads us away from

---

6. Reading the Bible isn't the same as meditating on God's Word, and it isn't all we need. Read Psalm 119 and count how many times this lover of the Word rejoices over simply *reading* it. I can't find any.

the gospel. But faith clings to Christ in everything and won't move an inch without his help (1 Cor. 15:10). Faith won't read a chapter, sing a hymn, say a prayer, or offer a gift without calling on the strength of Christ that the Spirit provides (Rom. 8:13). This is what it means to live by faith in the Son of God (Gal. 2:20). And when we live this way, God revives us.

I Am the Lord, Your Healer

Because we so easily decline and decay, God has given us great and precious promises of recovery—if we apply ourselves to using his means. In chapter 12, we glanced at a few of these promises. Now let's linger over one and see what we learn about spiritual healing.

> Return, O Israel, to the Lord your God,
>   for you have stumbled because of your iniquity.
> Take with you words
>   and return to the Lord;
> say to him,
>   "Take away all iniquity;
> accept what is good,
>   and we will pay with bulls
>   the vows of our lips.
> Assyria shall not save us;
>   we will not ride on horses;
> and we will say no more, 'Our God,'
>   to the work of our hands.
> In you the orphan finds mercy."
>
> I will heal their apostasy;
>   I will love them freely,
>   for my anger has turned from them.

I will be like the dew to Israel;
    he shall blossom like the lily;
    he shall take root like the trees of Lebanon;
his shoots shall spread out;
    his beauty shall be like the olive,
    and his fragrance like Lebanon.
They shall return and dwell beneath my shadow;
    they shall flourish like the grain;
they shall blossom like the vine;
    their fame shall be like the wine of Lebanon.

O Ephraim, what have I to do with idols?
    It is I who answer and look after you.
I am like an evergreen cypress;
    from me comes your fruit. (Hos. 14:1–8)

God doesn't abandon his wandering children but calls them to *return*. Hosea 13 tells us that most of the people addressed by the prophet above were under God's threat because of their wickedness —and it wasn't long after this that God made good his threat. Isn't this striking? Even in the middle of the extreme wickedness of his people, even in the same breath with which he threatens to dash their babies to the ground and rip open their pregnant women (Hos. 13:16), he offers his mercy. Remember that Jesus deals the same way with the church at Laodicea (Rev. 3:14–21). No one who belongs to God is beyond the reach of his grace.

In times of widespread apostasy, even true believers can be swept along by the sins of the masses and suffer spiritual decay: "And because lawlessness will be increased, the love of many will grow cold" (Matt. 24:12). This was happening to true Israelites, although they hadn't completely broken their covenant with God. He still called himself "the LORD your God," even though their sin was great.

parched and ravenous i seek him

When God plans to revive us, he calls us to use the means he has given us for our healing: "Take with you words and return to the Lord" (Hos. 14:2). That is, God calls us to renew our repentance; he calls us to *fervent* prayer.

Don't take your danger too lightly. Remember that we're dealing with God—and that "it is a fearful thing to fall into the hands of the living God" (Heb. 10:31). We should make a full confession and look for God's pardon for *all* our sins (Hos. 14:2). We mustn't hang onto even one pet sin or try to smuggle it into God's presence. He won't be fooled. Take every sin to him and ask for nothing but grace: "Receive us graciously" (Hos. 14:2). We must ask God to show us his mercy—to let us know, in our hearts, that he has accepted us.

Taking all our sins to God involves making our confession *specific*. Hosea said that Israel should confess her dependence on man and her idolatry (14:3). These were the popular sins of the day, and even faithful Israelites had been caught up in them. God expected a full confession.

Along with renewing our repentance, God expects us to renew our faith in him. In Hosea 14:3, he told Israel to confess his mercy as the foundation of their hope: "In you the orphan finds mercy." And out of renewed repentance and faith flow our praise and thanksgiving, which is the purpose for which God heals us: "Take away all iniquity; accept what is good, and we will pay with bulls the vows of our lips," our vows of praise (Hos. 14:2).

In fact, when God repairs our spiritual decay and heals our backsliding through these means, he does it to the praise of his own glory. That's why he prescribes these duties to us. Our obedience isn't the *cause* of the love and grace he then gives us to heal us, but he does require it—and in fact, through it, he dispenses his grace. As always in the Bible, there's a mysterious harmony between God's sovereign grace ("I will heal their apostasy; I will

192

love them freely"—v. 4) and our diligent duty ("Return"; "take with you words" vv. 1–2).

Since this is the way God deals with us, we can't expect to recover unless our hearts drive us to sincere prayer, thorough confession and repentance, fresh faith, and praise to God. We can't expect that, if we continue to be spiritually reckless, God will intervene, uninvited, to fix us. If he worked that way, without showing us our danger and convicting us of our sin, how would we ever know to thank him?

But we *should* thank him. Backsliding isn't a hangnail; it's a cancer that weakens our souls and will certainly destroy us if God doesn't heal us. Because the sin of backsliding is so dangerous, the Bible often calls recovery from it *healing* (see Ps. 6:2; Isa. 57:18–19; Hos. 6:1). In Hosea 14, this healing (v. 4) includes pardon of past sin and a new supply of grace to enable fruitful obedience (vv. 4–7). This healing flows only from God's grace (v. 4), and it flows like the mighty river of metaphors in verses 5–7 that paint a lavish picture of God's healing. This is what we can hope for, and expect, from our God.

Spiritual Renewal and the Glory of Christ

After spending chapter 12 asking the Spirit to search us and to tell us whether we're backsliders, it may feel like we've lost our focus on the glory of Christ. But when we answer the question "How do I recover from spiritual decay?" we find ourselves right back where we started this book. There can't be any real revival apart from beholding the glory of Christ.

Every Ounce of Grace that We Receive Comes from Jesus Christ

As we've seen in Hosea 14, the Old Testament promises grace; but the way we receive it is revealed in the New. Jesus assures us that without him we can't lift a finger. Like a branch that's been hacked away from the vine, apart from him we can't produce even the most shriveled piece of fruit (John 15:3–5). He's our head, and we're his body. Separate the two, and what do you have? He is our life, and he energizes every useful spiritual move we make (Gal. 2:20; Col. 3:1–4).

Are you at all stirred by a conviction that your spiritual life is languishing? Do you yearn for a renewal of spiritual strength that will cause your faith, love, and holiness to flourish? Then drive a stake into this solid rock: we won't have any bit of this apart from Jesus. We can claim every promise in the Book and muster our courage to carry out the toughest spiritual disciplines, but we won't find a breath of relief unless Christ breathes on us. And if only Christ can renew us, isn't he glorious?

Every Ounce of Grace that We Receive Comes through Faith

By faith we come to Christ, are planted in Christ, and abide in Christ so that we bear fruit for him. By our faith he works in us and acts in us, so that we live by faith in the Son of God. We won't find a whisper in the Scriptures to suggest that we'll receive anything from Christ unless it's through faith. Faith points away from us and our strength to Christ and his glory.

We Put This Faith in the Person of Christ

We end this book where we began: what we need, more than all the wisdom and wealth of the world, is a steady view of the glory of the Lamb who is revealed to us by faith in his Word. It's the only medicine that can heal our sick souls and the only true fountain of youth that keeps our spirits fresh in youth or old age. "Those who look to him are radiant, and their faces shall never be ashamed" (Ps. 34:5). What's a better expression of faith in Christ than to believe that looking at him will refresh us? Or what better work of faith than to look at his glory? Isn't this the ultimate confidence in him?

Spiritual Recovery Begins, and Continues, When We Gaze on Christ's Glory

A view of Christ's glory changes us into his image, more and more every day, through the mirror of the Scriptures, as we've already seen (2 Cor. 3:18). If you've ever been revived, it was because you had a clearer, more constant view of Christ. If you're ever going to be renewed again, it will happen when you see his glory. Haven't we tried enough religious gimmicks to prop up our faith? Isn't it time we turn our eyes once again to the One who saved us—and let his beauty overwhelm us? What would the church be like if all of us kept the eyes of our faith ever fixed on the glory of the Lamb?

May it be so with you.

May it be so with me.

As a Stranger

As a stranger here I wander
in a wasteland, vast and void,
worn and weary, pressing onward,
gazing at my Lord.
Parched and ravenous I seek him,
waiting, kneeling at his throne;
panting as a hart for water,
my heart pants for God alone.

May I dwell among the faithful
who delight themselves in Christ,
longing only for his presence,
seeking paradise.
Turn our eyes away from idols;
fix our vision on you, Lord;
may we only seek the treasure
of your holy, living Word.

Burning, yearning for my Jesus,
groaning in this mortal jail;
my soul is consumed with longing
till death removes the veil.
When we're clothed with him in heaven
we will see him face to face;
we will ever dwell before him,
brought there by his sovereign grace.

For Reflection and Discussion

1. One of the points we drew from Hosea 14 is that when his people are wallowing in unthinkable sin, God reaches out to them in their darkness and calls them back to himself. Think about some of the sins that people like Noah and Moses and Abraham and Samson and David and Peter fell into—and yet God held out his hands to them. How does this show his glory?

2. Describe in your own words how our hard work and God's sovereign mercy work together to bring our renewal.

3. How does our spiritual renewal bring glory and honor to Christ?

4. This is the final exam for the whole book: How does seeing the glory of Christ bring our spiritual renewal?

Also by Kris Lundgaard

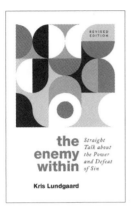

the enemy within *Straight Talk about the Power and Defeat of Sin*

Kris Lundgaard

the devoted mind *Seeking God's Face in a World of Distraction*

Kris Lundgaard

This revised edition of Kris Lundgaard's best-selling classic brings the wisdom of Puritan John Owen to a broad audience. Find insight, encouragement, and hope for your battle with sin.

"Kris Lundgaard has done the impossible. He has given us some of the best of Puritan theology in a language all of us can understand. This book will challenge you to radical spiritual transformation!"
—**Richard L. Pratt Jr.**, President, Third Millennium Ministries

Are you distracted, weary, and unresponsive to God's grace? Drawing on the wisdom of Puritan John Owen, Kris Lundgaard shows how to find life and peace by cultivating a spiritually devoted mind.

"Here is a book to be savored slowly. This is one of my most joyful devotional reads of recent years. If you want to grow in delight in Jesus and the knowledge of God, I warmly recommend it."
—**Christopher Ash**, Writer-in-Residence, Tyndale House, Cambridge

TRUTHFORLIFE®

THE BIBLE-TEACHING MINISTRY OF **ALISTAIR BEGG**

The mission of Truth For Life is to teach the Bible with clarity and relevance so that unbelievers will be converted, believers will be established, and local churches will be strengthened.

Daily Program

Each day, Truth For Life distributes the Bible teaching of Alistair Begg across the U.S. and in several locations outside of the U.S. through 2,000 radio outlets. To find a radio station near you, visit **truthforlife.org/stationfinder**.

Free Teaching

The daily program, and Truth For Life's entire teaching library of over 3,000 Bible-teaching messages, can be accessed for free online at **truthforlife.org** and through Truth For Life's mobile app, which can be download for free from your app store.

At-Cost Resources

Books and audio studies from Alistair Begg are available for purchase at cost, with no markup. Visit **truthforlife.org/store**.

Where to Begin?

If you're new to Truth For Life and would like to know where to begin listening and learning, find starting point suggestions at **truthforlife.org/firststep**. For a full list of ways to connect with Truth For Life, visit **truthforlife.org/subscribe**.

Contact Truth For Life

P.O. Box 398000 Cleveland, Ohio 44139

phone 1 (888) 588-7884   **email** letters@truthforlife.org truthforlife.org

Did you find this book helpful?
Consider writing a review online.
We appreciate your feedback!

Or write to P&R at editorial@prpbooks.com
with your comments. We'd love to hear from you.